THE DIVINE LITURGY OF SAINT JOHN CHRYSOSTOM

Η ΘΕΙΑ ΛΕΙΤΟΥΡΓΙΑ ΤΟΥ ΑΓΙΟΥ ΙΩΑΝΝΟΥ ΤΟΥ ΧΡΥΣΟΣΤΟΜΟΥ

A New Translation by Members
of the Faculty of Hellenic College/
Holy Cross Greek Orthodox School of Theology

HOLY CROSS ORTHODOX PRESS
Brookline, Massachusetts 02146

Published by Holy Cross Orthodox Press
50 Goddard Avenue
Brookline, Massachusetts 02146

Cover design by Mary C. Vaporis

Library of Congress Cataloging-in-Publication
Data

Greek Orthodox Archdiocese of North and
South America. The divine liturgy of Saint
John Chrysostom.

Translation of: Preface—Introduction to the
divine liturgy—The divine liturgy—[etc.]
1. Lord's Supper—Greek Orthodox Arch-
diocese of North and South America—Liturgy
—Texts. 2. Lord's Supper—Orthodox Eastern
Church—Liturgy—Texts. 3. Greek Orthodox
Archdiocese of North and South America—
Liturgy—Texts. 4. Orthodox Eastern Church—
Liturgy—Texts. I. Title.
BX375.L4A45 1985   264.019036   85-24746
ISBN 0-917651-17-0

THE DIVINE LITURGY
OF SAINT JOHN CHRYSOSTOM

Η ΘΕΙΑ ΛΕΙΤΟΥΡΓΙΑ
ΤΟΥ ΑΓΙΟΥ ΙΩΑΝΝΟΥ ΤΟΥ ΧΡΥΣΟΣΤΟΜΟΥ

THE LORD

CONTENTS

THE THEOTOKOS

PREFACE

Numerous English translations in use by the churches of our Archdiocese, featuring many differences among them, have often caused bewilderment and confusion among the faithful.

For this reason, His Eminence Archbishop Iakovos appointed a committee, composed of faculty members of Hellenic College/Holy Cross Greek Orthodox School of Theology, to produce a standard English translation using the modern language but faithful to the meaning of the original text.

It should be stated that we await with great anticipation the official approval of the translation of the Divine Liturgy by the members of the Holy Synod of our Archdiocese. Meanwhile, the present translation of the Divine Liturgy is offered as a "working translation" with the prayer and hope that its use in our churches will result in further improvements and refinements so that in the very near future we will share one English translation as we now do the same Greek text.

The principal translators were: Fathers Alkiviadis Calivas, Theodore Stylianopoulos, N. Michael Vaporis, Thomas FitzGerald, and Peter Chamberas. Offering important contributions were: Fr. George Papademetriou and Dr. Athan Anagnostopoulos. Assisting at various times were: Bishop Demetrios Trakatellis, Dr. George Bebis, Professor Ioanna Clarke, Fr. Stanley Harakas,

Dr. Elias Patsavos, Fr. John Travis, and Dr. Penelope Tzougros.

The text was sent to all the bishops of the Archdiocese for their review, comments, and contributions. In addition, the following received the translation and offered their valuable comments: Bishop Kallistos Ware, Bishop John Martin of blessed memory, Professors John Erikson, Veselin Kesich, Harry Magoulias, George Panichas, John Rexine, and Eva C. Topping; and Fathers Nicholas Apostola, Anthony Coniaris, Leonidas Contos, Demetrios Constantelos, George Gallos, Andrew Georgaroudakis, Anthony Kostouros, Frank Marangos, Andrew Missiras, Charles Sarelis, Robert Stephanopoulos, John Tavlarides, and Harry Vulopas. To all the participants, we express our thanks for their invaluable contributions.

Special thanks are also owed to Miss Georgia Stathopoulou and Miss Eleni Baker for their care in preparing the text for publication.

Above all, however, I must thank, on behalf of the members of the committee, His Eminence Archbishop Iakovos for permission to publish the present translation.

                                            Fr. N. Michael Vaporis

AN INTRODUCTION TO
THE DIVINE LITURGY

HISTORY AND OUTLINE

The Word Divine Liturgy

The Divine Liturgy is the sacred rite by which the Orthodox Church celebrates the mystery of the Eucharist. This title for the Eucharist is derived from two Greek words *theia* and *leitourgia*. The word *theia* means pertaining to God, hence divine. The word *leitourgia* comes from two words *leitos,* which means people, and *ergon,* which means work, hence the work of the people or a public service, act or function. The word *leitourgia* was used in Greek antiquity to describe those services and acts which were performed for the benefit and common interest of all, including acts of worship. It was in this latter religious sense that the word found its way into the vocabulary of Scripture and the Church. In the Septuagint (the Greek translation of the Old Testament) the word was applied to the Temple services and the functions of the priests. In the New Testament, where the word appears infrequently, it describes the saving work of Christ (Heb 8.6) and Christian worship (Acts 13.21). In the Apostolic Fathers and later tradition the word was applied to worship. By the fourth century, the word *leitourgia,* together with the adjective *theia* (i.e. Divine Liturgy), had become the technical term for the mystery of the Eucharist. The word Eucharist in turn means thanksgiving. It takes its name from the great prayer of consecration (the Anaphora) recited by the celebrant of the Divine Liturgy.

The Origins of the Divine Liturgy

The Divine Liturgy is composed of two parts. The first part of the Liturgy is the Liturgy of the Word, also called the Synaxis or the Proanaphora. Sometimes this part has been referred to as the Liturgy of the Catechumens. The second part is the Eucharist, which has also been called the Liturgy of the Faithful. The Liturgy of the Word in its basic, classical shape is a Christianized version of the synagogue service focusing on the reading of a biblical passage and the homily. The Eucharist on the other hand is derived from the words and actions of the Lord at the Mystical (Last) Supper.

The connection of the Divine Liturgy to the prayer service of the synagogue and to a Jewish household or fraternal ritual meal must be understood against the backdrop of the nascent Christian community. The Lord, His apostles and the first Christians were Jews. It is clear that the Church is characterized forever by its Semitic origins. It is equally clear that the Church has close connections with Hellenism. The Church was born in Jerusalem, but grew up within the Hellenistic civilization. Her liturgy, art, and theology are radiant with the imperishable traces of this double experience. Louis Bouyer observes: "It is true that the Christian liturgy, and the Eucharist especially, is one of the most original creations of Christianity. But however original it is, it is not a sort of an ex nihilo creation. To think so is to condemn ourselves to a minimal understanding of it.''.

The Eucharist itself was instituted by Christ at the supper on Holy Thursday to perpetuate the remembrance (*anamnesis*) of His redemptive work and to establish a continuous intimate communion (*koinonia*) between Himself and those who believe in Him. The actions and words of the Lord concerning the bread and wine formed the basis for the Eucharist, the chief recurrent liturgical rite of the Church. The nucleus of every eucharistic rite consists in four actions: the offering and the placing of bread and wine on the holy Table; the *anaphora* or great eucharist prayer, which includes the words of institution and the invocation of the Holy Spirit for the consecration of the gifts; the breaking of the consecrated Bread (an act called the fraction); and the communion of the consecrated gifts by the people of God.

At first the Eucharist was celebrated within the context of an evening community meal, referred to as the *agape* or love feast. By the end of the first or the beginning of the second century, the celebration of the Eucharist was separated from the community meal and transposed to the early morning hours.

The Development of the Divine Liturgy

The Divine Liturgy is a complex act of movement, sound, and sights characterized by a deep sense of harmony, beauty, dignity, and mystery. It is structured around two solemn entrances, which today are abbreviated forms of earlier more elaborate ceremonies, the reading and the exposition of Holy Scripture, the great eucharistic prayer (the Anaphora), and the distribution of Holy Communion. Elaborate opening rites (*enarxis*) and a series of dismissal rites (*apolysis*) embrace the whole action.

The first or Little Entrance, the entry of the clergy and the people into the Church, once marked the beginning of the Liturgy of the Word. The Little Entrance is a solemn procession with the Gospel accompanied with entrance hymns.

The second or Great Entrance once marked the beginning of the Eucharist. It is a solemn procession with the gifts of the bread and wine that are to be offered and consecrated. These gifts are brought to the Church by the people. The elements used for the offering are prepared by the clergy. During the course of the eighth century, this rite of preparation was transferred from before the Great Entrance to a time before the *enarxis* of the Divine Liturgy. This service is called the Proskomide and it is performed at the Table of Preparation called the Prothesis. It is here, after the preparation of the bread and the cup and the commemoration of the saints, that the celebrant also remembers the faithful, both living and dead by name.

The verbal and non-verbal elements of the Divine Liturgy are fitted together harmoniously, so as to weave a pattern of prayer that addresses and inspires the whole person, body and soul. The principle behind the development of its ceremonial splendor rests upon the notion that our earthly worship reflects the joy and majesty of heavenly worship.

On the verbal side of the Liturgy we hear: eloquent prayers of praise, thanksgiving, intercession, and confession; litanies, petitions, acclamations, greetings, and invitations; hymns, chants, psalmody, and creedal statements; and intoned scriptural readings and a homily. On the non-verbal side, we are involved with solemn processions and an assortment of liturgical gestures. The eyes are filled with the actions of the servers, as well as with the sights of the Lord and His saints gazing at us from the icons. The nostrils are filled with the fragrance of incense and the heart is grasped by the profound silence of the divine presence. People touch hands gently, saying, "Christ is in our midst," when called upon to love one another before the offering of the gifts as a sign of mutual forgiveness and love. With one voice and heart they recite the Creed, and recommit themselves to the fulness of the truth of the Orthodox faith. Participating in Holy Communion, the faithful taste and see that the Lord is good.

The basic outline of the Divine Liturgy goes

back to the New Testament. Ritual and text evolved gradually; the several elements of the Liturgy developed unevenly and at different stages. Its structures were expanded, augmented and adorned with chants, prayers, and various ceremonials. By the tenth century, the eucharistic rites of Constantinople, the chief see of the Orthodox East, had become more or less crystallized. The process of growth, modification, and adaptation has been relatively slow ever since. By virtue of its prestige, the rites of Constantinople first influenced and finally replaced all other rites in the Orthodox East. Since the end of the twelfth century, with minor variations that reflect local customs, the Liturgy of Constantinople has become the common rite of all Orthodox Churches.

The Three Liturgies

Constantinople was the magnificent crucible in which several liturgical traditions converged. Out of this synthesis came three liturgies, which were distinctly Constantinopolitan. Firmly rooted in God's written word and strongly influenced by the patristic experience, these liturgies take us to the heart of God's glory and philanthropia.

The Liturgy of Saint Basil was, until the twelfth century, the chief liturgy of Constantinople. Its anaphora is probably the most eloquent of all liturgies, east and west. Powerful in its unity of thought, theological depth and rich biblical imagery, it was celebrated every Sunday and great feast day. Now it is used only ten times during the year: on the five Sundays of the Great Fast; on the vigils of Pascha, Christmas, and Epiphany; on Holy Thursday and on the Feast of Saint Basil, January 1.

The Liturgy of Saint John Chrysostomos is shorter and less rhetorical than that of Saint Basil. It is distinguished for its simplicity and clarity. At first it was probably the weekday liturgy of Constantinople. Gradually it superseded and replaced the Liturgy of Saint Basil. The Liturgy of Saint John Chrysostomos is now celebrated at every eucharistic assembly unless the Liturgy of Saint Basil or the Liturgy of the Pre-Sanctified Gifts is to be celebrated.

The Liturgy of the Pre-Sanctified Gifts is not a full Divine Liturgy in that it does not contain the anaphora. This liturgy is now used on Wednesdays and Fridays of the Great Fast and on the first three days of Holy Week. It is comprised of Vespers, the solemn transfer to the holy Table of the elements of Holy Communion consecrated at the Divine Liturgy the previous Sunday or Saturday, and the order of the distribution of Holy Communion as in the other liturgies.

According to local custom, three other ancient liturgies are also used by Orthodox Churches on the occasion of the feast day of the saints to which their authorship is traditionally attributed. These are the liturgies of Saint James (Iakovos), the ancient liturgy of Jerusalem; Saint Mark, the ancient liturgy of Alexandria; and Saint Gregory the Theologian, an ancient liturgy of Cappadocia and Alexandria.

The Celebrants of the Divine Liturgy

The Divine Liturgy is a corporate action of the whole people of God. The clergy and the laity together constitute the one, living, divine-human organism, the Body of Christ, the Church. The eucharistic assembly presupposes the presence and active participation of clergy and laity, each with their own essential and distinctive ministry, role, and function. Together they enter into the depths of the divine light, in accordance to the measure of the faith given them by God and the purity of their heart.

The chief celebrant of the Eucharist is the bishop or, in his absence, the presbyter, without whom there can be no Eucharist. The bishop or priest acts in the place of Christ who is the true priest and celebrant of the eucharistic mystery. Christ Himself is the one Who offers and is offered, the one Who receives and distributes. Through His perfect self-offering, as the unique High Priest and mediator of the New Covenant, Christ continues to unite redeemed humanity to God (Heb 9.11-15; 10.10).

Reception of Holy Communion

The Eucharist belongs to and is shared by those who have been baptized into the Church and who hold a common faith in the bond of love. Thus, only those Orthodox Christians in full communion with the Church may partake of the Holy Gifts. For the Orthodox, the Eucharist is not an instrument for achieving Christian unity, but the very sign and crowning of that union based on doctrinal truths and canonical harmony already held and possessed in common. The Eucharist is both a celebration and a confession of the faith of the Church. Hence it is not possible to approach Holy Communion by way of hospitality.

It is expected that every baptized and chrismated Orthodox adult, child, and infant be regular and frequent recipients of the Divine Mysteries. It is presupposed that adult and children communicants have fasted from the evening meal prior to receiving Holy Communion at the morning Eucharist.

Care must be taken that one approaches Holy Communion with spiritual discernment. Saint Nicholas Kabasilas teaches: "Let not everyone come to receive it, but only those who are worthy, 'for the holy gifts are for the holy people of God.' Those whom the priest calls holy are *not only* those who have attained perfection, *but also* those who are striving for it without having yet obtained it . . . That is why Christians, if they have not committed such sins (mortal sins) as would cut them off from Christ and bring death, are in no way prevented, when partaking of the holy mysteries, from receiving sanctification . . . For no one has holiness of himself; it is not the consequence of human virtue, but comes for all from Him and through Him."

For the faithful the Divine Liturgy is experienced at one and the same time as judgment, forgiveness, and true life. In every Liturgy people hear the good news of Christ and enter into a process of conversion. Repentance is offered as a way of life, a continuous journey toward God the Father. We learn to live in communion with Christ not only in the moments of the Liturgy, but in the exierences of daily life. Repentance becomes a way of life, a continuous journey toward God the Father.

In the Divine Liturgy we share in the power of the resurrection, which alone liberates and transfigures all of life and makes possible the reconstruction of all order, personal and social.

Every liturgy is an opportunity for a new dynamic encounter with the Holy Trinity for the renewal and sanctification of human persons and creation.

THEOLOGICAL MEANING

The Eucharist or Divine Liturgy is the central mystery of the Church. It is at once the source and the summit of her life. In it the Church is continuously changed from a human community to the body of Christ, the temple of the Holy Spirit, and the holy people of God. The Eucharist, according to Saint Nicholas Kabasilas, is the final and greatest of the mysteries "since it is not possible to go beyond it or add anything to it. After the Eucharist there is nowhere further to go. There all must stand, and try to examine the means by which we may preserve the treasure to the end. For in it we obtain God Himself, and God is united with us in the most perfect union."

Every sacred mystery makes its partakers into members of Christ. But the Eucharist effects this perfectly. To quote Saint Nicholas Kabasilas again: "By dispensation of His grace, He (Christ) disseminates Himself in every believer through that flesh whose substance comes from bread and wine, blending Himself with the bodies of believers, to secure by this union with the Immortal that man, too, may be a sharer in incorruption. He gives these gifts by virtue of the benediction through which He transelements the natural quality of these visible things to that immortal thing."

Through the Eucharist divine life flows into us and penetrates the fabric of our humanity. The future life is infused into the present one and is blended with it, so that our fallen humanity may be transformed into the glorified humanity of the new Adam, Christ. The Eucharist is our "medicine of immortality and the antidote against death, enabling us to live forever in Jesus Christ," according to Saint Ignatios.

The Messianic Banquet

In this present age between the two comings of Jesus Christ our Lord, the Divine Liturgy is always the messianic banquet, the meal of the kingdom, the time and place in which the heavenly joins and mingles with the earthly. The Eucharist initiates humankind, nature, and time into the mystery of the uncreated Trinity. The Divine Liturgy is not simply a sacred drama or a mere representation of past events. It constitutes the very presence of God's embracing love, which purifies, enlightens, perfects, and deifies (2 Pet 1.4) all those who are invited to the marriage supper of the Lamb (Rev 19.9), all who through baptism and chrismation have been incorporated into the Church and have become Christ-bearers and Spirit-bearers.

In the Divine Liturgy we do not commemorate one or another isolated event of sacred history. We celebrate, in joy and thanksgiving, the whole mystery of the divine economy from creation to incarnation, especially, in the words of the Liturgy, "the cross, the tomb, the resurrection on the third day, the ascension into heaven, the enthronement at the right hand of the Father, and the second glorious coming." Thus, in experiencing the risen and reigning Christ in the Divine Liturgy, the past, present, and future of the history of salvation are lived as one reality.

A Continuous Pentecost

Each Divine Liturgy is a continuation of the mystery of Pentecost. It is the renewal and the confirmation of the coming of the Holy Spirit who is ever present in the Church. In the Divine Liturgy of Saint John Chrysostomos we pray: "Make us worthy to find grace in Your presence so that our sacrifice may be pleasing to You and that Your good and gracious Spirit may abide with us and with the gifts here presented and with all Your people." The worshiping community prays earnestly that it may continue to be Spirit-bearing and that the consecrated gifts may become a "communion of the

Holy Spirit.'' The faithful receive Holy Communion for the forgiveness of sins and life eternal, two gifts of divine love, so that they may find mercy and grace with all the saints, who throughout the ages have been pleasing to God. Through the celebration of the Divine Liturgy sin, corruption, and death, the divisive and destructive powers of Satan, are abolished. In the Eucharist all things are united with God. In the changed elements of the bread and wine, creation, freed from the bondage of corruption, becomes itself Spirit-bearing.

Partakers of Divine Nature

Through the power of God the bread and wine of the Liturgy are changed into the very Body and Blood of Christ. This change is not physical but mystical and sacramental. While the qualities of the bread and wine remain, we partake of the true Body and Blood of Christ

The Eucharist, so writes Saint Ignatios, ''is the flesh of our Savior Jesus Christ, the flesh which suffered for our sins and which the Father in His graciousness raised from the dead.'' In the Eucharist we are offered Christ's deified flesh, to which we are joined, without confusion or division, in order to partake of divine life. In the Eucharist, Christ acts to make us His own Body. According to Saint Nicholas Kabasilas, ''the Bread of Life Himself changes him who feeds on Him and transforms and asimilates him into Himself.'' Thus, eternity penetrates our finitude. In the words of Saint

Gregory Palamas, "by this flesh [of Christ in the Eucharist] our community is raised to heaven; that is where this Bread truly dwells; and we enter into the Holy of Holies by the pure offering of the Body of Christ." Men, women, and children are invited to share in the trinitarian life of God. The life of the Trinity flows and dwells in us through "the grace of our Lord Jesus Christ and the love of God the Father and the communion of the Holy Spirit" (2 Cor 13-14). We become God-bearers.

The Local Church

The mystery of the Church as the Body of Christ is fully realized in the Divine Liturgy, for the Eucharist is Christ crucified and risen, in His personal presence. Every local church, living in full the sacramental life, according to John Meyendorff, is the "miracle of the new life in Christ lived in community and is built upon and around the Table of the Lord. Whenever and wherever the Divine Liturgy is celebrated, in the context of doctrinal unity and canonical norms, the local church possesses the mark of the true Church of God: unity, holiness, catholicity, and apostolicity. These marks cannot belong to any human gathering; they are the eschatological signs given to a community through the Spirit of God."

A Vision of the True Life and the New Humanity

The Eucharist is a network of relations, a community. It unites the members of the Church both to Christ and to one another. "Because there is one bread, we who are many are one body, for we all partake of the one bread" (1 Cor 10.17). Sharing in the life of Christ and energized by the gifts of the Holy Spirit, the Church becomes an epiphany of divine love. Saint John of Damascus writes: "If union is in truth with Christ and with one another, we are assuredly also united voluntarily with all those who partake with us." The Eucharist becomes the vision and the image of true human life as God created it and intended it to become. Through the Eucharist the destructive powers of Satan are being continuously defeated and the life of selfless love is being revealed, learned. According to Vladimir Lossky, the Divine Liturgy makes manifest the true dimensions of the Christian life as "the way which leads from the multiplicity of corruption, that of individuals which divide humanity, towards the unity of the one, pure nature in which there is disclosed a new multiplicity: that of persons united to God in the Holy Spirit."

In and through the Divine Liturgy all are initiated into the depths of the corporate life of the Church as communion with God. Here we have a glimpse of the Church as an image of the Holy Trinity. To quote Lossky again, there is "a single human nature in the hypostasis of Christ, many human hypostases in the grace of the Holy Spirit." The eucharistic assembly becomes the image of the new humanity gathered around the risen Lord, empowered, nourished, and perfected by His love and mercy.

The eucharistic assembly in its communal and ecclesial character is the eschatological community of God, a community which experiences the new age in Christ and witnesses to the presence of God's Kingdom in history. In the words of John Zizioulas: "At the Divine Liturgy we subsist in a manner different from the biological, as members of a body which transcends every exclusiveness of a biological or social kind. In such an ecclesial identity we appear to exist not as that which we are, but as that which we will become, not as a result of an evolution of the human race, whether biological or historical, but as the result of the victory of Christ."

Fr. Alkiviades Calivas

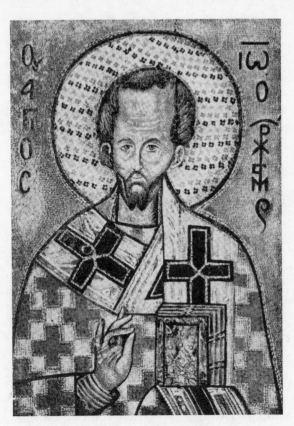

SAINT JOHN CHRYSOSTOMOS

Η ΘΕΙΑ ΛΕΙΤΟΥΡΓΙΑ ΤΟΥ ΑΓΙΟΥ ΙΩΑΝΝΟΥ ΤΟΥ ΧΡΥΣΟΣΤΟΜΟΥ

Ἱερεύς: Εὐλογημένη ἡ βασιλεία τοῦ Πατρὸς καὶ τοῦ Υἱοῦ καὶ τοῦ Ἁγίου Πνεύματος, νῦν καὶ ἀεὶ καὶ εἰς τοὺς αἰῶνας τῶν αἰώνων.

Λαός: **Ἀμήν.**

ΤΑ ΑΝΤΙΦΩΝΑ

Η ΜΕΓΑΛΗ ΣΥΝΑΠΤΗ

* *Ἱερεύς:* Ἐν εἰρήνῃ τοῦ Κυρίου δεηθῶμεν.

Λαός: **Κύριε, ἐλέησον.**

* *Ἱερεύς:* Ὑπὲρ τῆς ἄνωθεν εἰρήνης καὶ τῆς σωτηρίας τῶν ψυχῶν ἡμῶν, τοῦ Κυρίου δεηθῶμεν.

Λαός: **Κύριε, ἐλέησον.**

* *Ἱερεύς:* Ὑπὲρ τῆς εἰρήνης τοῦ σύμπαντος κόσμου, εὐσταθείας τῶν ἁγίων τοῦ Θεοῦ Ἐκκλησιῶν καὶ τῆς τῶν πάντων ἑνώσεως, τοῦ Κυρίου δεηθῶμεν.

Λαός: **Κύριε, ἐλέησον.**

**Τὰ μέρη τῆς Λειτουργίας τὰ ὁποῖα ἀνήκουν εἰς τὸν διάκονον σημειοῦνται διὰ ἀστερίσκου.*

1

THE DIVINE LITURGY OF
SAINT JOHN CHRYSOSTOM

Priest: Blessed is the kingdom of the Father and the Son and the Holy Spirit, now and forever and to the ages of ages.

People: **Amen.**

THE ANTIPHONS

THE GREAT LITANY

**Priest:* In peace let us pray to the Lord.

People: **Lord, have mercy.**

**Priest:* For the peace of God and the salvation of our souls, let us pray to the Lord.

People: **Lord, have mercy.**

**Priest:* For peace in the whole world, for the stability of the holy churches of God, and for the unity of all, let us pray to the Lord.

People: **Lord, have mercy.**

**The parts of the Liturgy belonging to the deacon are marked with an asterisk.*

1

*Ἱερεύς: Ὑπὲρ τοῦ ἁγίου οἴκου τούτου καὶ τῶν μετὰ πίστεως, εὐλαβείας καὶ φόβου Θεοῦ εἰσιόντων ἐν αὐτῷ, τοῦ Κυρίου δεηθῶμεν.

Λαός: **Κύριε, ἐλέησον.**

*Ἱερεύς: Ὑπὲρ τοῦ Ἀρχιεπισκόπου ἡμῶν (Ὄνομα) καὶ τοῦ Ἐπισκόπου ἡμῶν (Ὄνομα), τοῦ τιμίου πρεσβυτερίου, τῆς ἐν Χριστῷ διακονίας, παντὸς τοῦ κλήρου καὶ τοῦ λαοῦ, τοῦ Κυρίου δεηθῶμεν.

Λαός: **Κύριε, ἐλέησον.**

*Ἱερεύς: Ὑπὲρ τοῦ εὐσεβοῦς ἡμῶν ἔθνους, πάσης ἀρχῆς καὶ ἐξουσίας ἐν αὐτῷ, τοῦ Κυρίου δεηθῶμεν.

Λαός: **Κύριε, ἐλέησον.**

*Ἱερεύς: Ὑπὲρ τῆς κοινότητος καὶ τῆς πόλεως ταύτης, πάσης πόλεως καὶ χώρας καὶ τῶν πίστει οἰκούντων ἐν αὐταῖς, τοῦ Κυρίου δεηθῶμεν.

Λαός: **Κύριε, ἐλέησον.**

*Ἱερεύς: Ὑπὲρ εὐκρασίας ἀέρων, εὐφορίας τῶν καρπῶν τῆς γῆς καὶ καιρῶν εἰρηνικῶν, τοῦ Κυρίου δεηθῶμεν.

Λαός: **Κύριε, ἐλέησον.**

Priest: For this holy house and for those who enter it with faith, reverence, and the fear of God, let us pray to the Lord.

People: **Lord, have mercy.**

Priest: For our Archbishop (*Name*), our Bishop (*Name*), the honorable presbyters, the deacons in the service of Christ, and all the clergy and laity, let us pray to the Lord.

People: **Lord, have mercy.**

Priest: For our country, the president, and all those in public service, let us pray to the Lord.

People: **Lord, have mercy.**

Priest: For this parish and city, for every city and country, and for the faithful who live in them, let us pray to the Lord.

People: **Lord, have mercy.**

Priest: For favorable weather, an abundance of the fruits of the earth, and temperate seasons, let us pray to the Lord.

Priest: **Lord, have mercy.**

Ἱερεύς: Ὑπὲρ πλεόντων, ὁδοιπορούντων, νοσούντων, καμνόντων, αἰχμαλώτων καὶ τῆς σωτηρίας αὐτῶν, τοῦ Κυρίου δεηθῶμεν.

Λαός: **Κύριε, ἐλέησον.**

Ἱερεύς: Ὑπὲρ τοῦ ῥυσθῆναι ἡμᾶς ἀπὸ πάσης θλίψεως, ὀργῆς, κινδύνου καὶ ἀνάγκης, τοῦ Κυρίου δεηθῶμεν.

Λαός: **Κύριε, ἐλέησον.**

Ἱερεύς: Ἀντιλαβοῦ, σῶσον, ἐλέησον καὶ διαφύλαξον ἡμᾶς, ὁ Θεός, τῇ σῇ χάριτι.

Λαός: **Κύριε, ἐλέησον.**

Ἱερεύς: Τῆς παναγίας, ἀχράντου, ὑπερευλογημένης, ἐνδόξου, δεσποίνης ἡμῶν Θεοτόκου καὶ ἀειπαρθένου Μαρίας, μετὰ πάντων τῶν ἁγίων μνημονεύσαντες, ἑαυτοὺς καὶ ἀλλήλους καὶ πᾶσαν τὴν ζωὴν ἡμῶν Χριστῷ τῷ Θεῷ παραθώμεθα.

Λαός: **Σοί, Κύριε.**

Ἱερεύς (χαμηλοφώνως): Κύριε ὁ Θεὸς ἡμῶν, οὗ τὸ κράτος ἀνείκαστον καὶ ἡ δόξα ἀκατάληπτος· οὗ τὸ ἔλεος ἀμέτρητον καὶ ἡ φιλανθρωπία ἄφατος· αὐτὸς Δέσποτα, κατὰ τὴν εὐσπλαγχνίαν σου, ἐπίβλεψον ἐφ' ἡμᾶς καὶ ἐπὶ τὸν ἅγιον οἶκον τοῦτον καὶ ποίησον μεθ' ἡμῶν καὶ τῶν συνευχομένων ἡμῖν πλούσια τὰ ἐλέη

Priest: For travelers by land, sea, and air, for the sick, the suffering, the captives, and for their salvation, let us pray to the Lord.

People: **Lord, have mercy.**

Priest: For our deliverance from all affliction, wrath, danger, and distress, let us pray to the Lord.

People: **Lord, have mercy.**

Priest: Help us, save us, have mercy upon us, and protect us, O God, by Your grace.

People: **Lord, have mercy.**

Priest: Remembering our most holy, pure, blessed, and glorious Lady, the Theotokos and ever virgin Mary, with all the saints, let us commit ourselves and one another and our whole life to Christ our God.

People: **To You, O Lord.**

Priest (in a low voice): Lord, our God, whose power is beyond compare, and glory is beyond understanding; whose mercy is boundless, and love for us is ineffable: look upon us and upon this holy house in Your compassion. Grant to us and to those who pray with us Your abundant

σου καὶ τοὺς οἰκτιρμούς σου.

Ἱερεύς: Ὅτι πρέπει σοι πᾶσα δόξα, τιμὴ καὶ προσκύνησις, τῷ Πατρὶ καὶ τῷ Υἱῷ καὶ τῷ Ἁγίῳ Πνεύματι, νῦν καὶ ἀεὶ καὶ εἰς τοὺς αἰῶνας τῶν αἰώνων.

Λαός: **Ἀμήν.**

ΤΟ ΠΡΩΤΟΝ ΑΝΤΙΦΩΝΟΝ

(Καὶ ψάλλεται τὸ Α΄ Ἀντίφωνον, συνοδευόμενον ἀπὸ τὸ ἐφύμνιον·)

Λαός: **Ταῖς πρεσβείαις τῆς Θεοτόκου, Σῶτερ, σῶσον ἡμᾶς** (3).

* *Ἱερεύς:* Ἔτι καὶ ἔτι ἐν εἰρήνῃ τοῦ Κυρίου δεηθῶμεν.

Λαός: **Κύριε, ἐλέησον.**

* *Ἱερεύς:* Ἀντιλαβοῦ, σῶσον, ἐλέησον καὶ διαφύλαξον ἡμᾶς, ὁ Θεός, τῇ σῇ χάριτι.

Λαός: **Κύριε, ἐλέησον.**

* *Ἱερεύς:* Τῆς παναγίας, ἀχράντου, ὑπερευλογημένης, ἐνδόξου, δεσποίνης ἡμῶν Θεοτόκου καὶ ἀειπαρθένου Μαρίας, μετὰ πάντων τῶν ἁγίων μνημονεύσαντες, ἑαυτοὺς καὶ ἀλλήλους καὶ πᾶσαν τὴν ζωὴν ἡμῶν Χριστῷ τῷ Θεῷ παραθώμεθα.

mercy.

Priest: For to You belong all glory, honor, and worship to the Father and the Son and the Holy Spirit, now and forever and to the ages of ages.

People: **Amen.**

THE FIRST ANTIPHON

(*The designated verses from the Psalms are sung with the hymn:*)

People: **By the intercessions of the Theotokos, Savior, save us** (*3*).

*Priest: In peace let us again pray to the Lord.

People: **Lord, have mercy.**

*Priest: Help us, save us, have mercy upon us, and protect us, O God, by Your grace.

People: **Lord, have mercy.**

*Priest: Remembering our most holy, pure, blessed, and glorious Lady, the Theotokos and ever virgin Mary, with all the saints, let us commit ourselves and one another, and our whole life to Christ our God.

Λαός: **Σοί, Κύριε.**

Ἱερεύς (χαμηλοφώνως): Κύριε ὁ Θεὸς ἡμῶν, σῶσον τὸν λαόν σου καὶ εὐλόγησον τὴν κληρονομίαν σου· τὸ πλήρωμα τῆς Ἐκκλησίας σου φύλαξον· ἁγίασον τοὺς ἀγαπῶντας τὴν εὐπρέπειαν τοῦ οἴκου σου· σὺ αὐτοὺς ἀντιδόξασον τῇ θεϊκῇ σου δυνάμει καὶ μὴ ἐγκαταλίπῃς ἡμᾶς τοὺς ἐλπίζοντας ἐπὶ σέ.

Ἱερεύς: Ὅτι σὸν τὸ κράτος καὶ σοῦ ἐστιν ἡ βασιλεία καὶ ἡ δύναμις καὶ ἡ δόξα τοῦ Πατρὸς καὶ τοῦ Υἱοῦ καὶ τοῦ Ἁγίου Πνεύματος, νῦν καὶ ἀεὶ καὶ εἰς τοὺς αἰῶνας τῶν αἰώνων.

Λαός: **Ἀμήν.**

ΤΟ ΔΕΥΤΕΡΟΝ ΑΝΤΙΦΩΝΟΝ

(Καὶ ψάλλεται τὸ Β΄. Ἀντίφωνον συνοδευόμενον ἀπὸ τὸ ἐφύμνιον·)

Λαός: **Σῶσον ἡμᾶς, Υἱὲ Θεοῦ, ὁ ἀναστὰς ἐκ νεκρῶν,**[1] **ψάλλοντάς σοι· Ἀλληλούϊα** (3).

Δόξα Πατρὶ καὶ Υἱῷ καὶ Ἁγίῳ Πνεύματι, καὶ νῦν καὶ ἀεὶ καὶ εἰς τοὺς αἰῶνας τῶν αἰώνων. Ἀμήν.

---

[1] Εἰς τὰς καθημερινὰς ψάλλεται τό: «ὁ ἐν ἁγίοις θαυμαστός».

People: **To You, O Lord.**

Priest (in a low voice): Lord our God, save Your people and bless Your inheritance; protect the whole body of Your Church; sanctify those who love the beauty of Your house; glorify them in return by Your divine power; and do not forsake us who hope in You.

Priest: For Yours is the dominion, the kingdom, the power, and the glory of the Father and the Son and the Holy Spirit, now and forever and to the ages of ages.

People: **Amen.**

THE SECOND ANTIPHON

(*The designated verses from the Psalms are sung with the hymn:*)

People: **Save us, O Son of God,
(who rose from the dead),**[1]
to You we sing: Alleluia (*3*).

Glory to the Father and the Son and the Holy Spirit, now and forever and to the ages of ages. Amen.

---

[1] *On weekdays we sing ("who are wondrous among Your saints").*

Ὁ μονογενὴς Υἱὸς καὶ Λόγος τοῦ Θεοῦ ἀθάνατος ὑπάρχων, καὶ καταδεξάμενος διὰ τὴν ἡμετέραν σωτηρίαν σαρκωθῆναι ἐκ τῆς ἁγίας Θεοτόκου καὶ ἀειπαρθένου Μαρίας, ἀτρέπτως ἐνανθρωπήσας· σταυρωθείς τε, Χριστὲ ὁ Θεός, θανάτῳ θάνατον πατήσας· εἷς ὢν τῆς Ἁγίας Τριάδος, συνδοξαζόμενος τῷ Πατρὶ καὶ τῷ Ἁγίῳ Πνεύματι, σῶσον ἡμᾶς.

* *Ἱερεύς:* Ἔτι καὶ ἔτι ἐν εἰρήνῃ τοῦ Κυρίου δεηθῶμεν.

Λαός: **Κύριε, ἐλέησον.**

* *Ἱερεύς:* Ἀντιλαβοῦ, σῶσον, ἐλέησον καὶ διαφύλαξον ἡμᾶς, ὁ Θεός, τῇ σῇ χάριτι.

Λαός: **Κύριε, ἐλέησον.**

* *Ἱερεύς:* Τῆς παναγίας, ἀχράντου ὑπερευλογημένης ἐνδόξου, δεσποίνης ἡμῶν Θεοτόκου καὶ ἀειπαρθένου Μαρίας, μετὰ πάντων τῶν ἁγίων μνημονεύσαντες, ἑαυτοὺς καὶ ἀλλήλους καὶ πᾶσαν τὴν ζωὴν ἡμῶν Χριστῷ τῷ Θεῷ παραθώμεθα.

Λαός: **Σοί, Κύριε.**

Ὁ τὰς κοινὰς ταύτας καὶ συμφώνους ἡμῖν χαρισάμενος προσευχάς, ὁ καὶ δυσὶ καὶ τρισὶ συμφωνοῦσιν ἐπὶ τῷ ὀνόματί σου, τὰς αἰτήσεις παρέχειν ἐπαγγειλάμενος· αὐτὸς καὶ νῦν τῶν

Only begotten Son and Word of God, although immortal You humbled Yourself for our salvation, taking flesh from the holy Theotokos and ever virgin Mary and, without change, becoming man. Christ, our God, You were crucified but conquered death by death. You are one of the Holy Trinity, glorified with the Father and the Holy Spirit—save us.

Priest: In peace let us again pray to the Lord.

People: **Lord, have mercy.**

Priest: Help us, save us, have mercy upon us, and protect us, O God, by Your grace.

People: **Lord, have mercy.**

Priest: Remembering our most holy, pure, blessed, and glorious Lady, the Theotokos and ever virgin Mary, with all the saints, let us commit ourselves and one another, and our whole life to Christ our God.

People: **To You, O Lord.**

Priest (in a low voice): Lord, You have given us grace to offer these common prayers with one heart. You have promised to grant the requests of two or three gathered in Your name. Fulfill

δούλων σου τὰ αἰτήματα πρὸς τὸ συμφέρον
πλήρωσον, χορηγῶν ἡμῖν ἐν τῷ παρόντι αἰῶνι
τὴν ἐπίγνωσιν τῆς σῆς ἀληθείας καὶ ἐν τῷ μέλ-
λοντι ζωὴν αἰώνιον χαριζόμενος.

Ἱερεύς: ῞Οτι ἀγαθὸς καὶ φιλάνθρωπος Θεὸς
ὑπάρχεις, καὶ σοὶ τὴν δόξαν ἀναπέμπομεν,
τῷ Πατρὶ καὶ τῷ Υἱῷ καὶ τῷ ῾Αγίῳ Πνεύματι,
νῦν καὶ ἀεὶ καὶ εἰς τοὺς αἰῶνας τῶν αἰώνων.

Λαός: **᾽Αμήν.**

ΤΟ ΤΡΙΤΟΝ ΑΝΤΙΦΩΝΟΝ

*(Καὶ ψάλλεται τὸ Γ΄ ᾽Αντίφωνον συνοδευόμενον
ἀπὸ τὸ ᾽Απολυτίκιον·)*

Η ΜΙΚΡΑ ΕΙΣΟΔΟΣ

*(Ψαλλομένου τοῦ ᾽Απολυτικίου, γίνεται ὑπὸ τοῦ
῾Ιερέως ἡ Εἴσοδος μετὰ τοῦ Εὐαγγελίου. ῾Ο ῾Ιερεὺς
προσεύχεται χαμηλοφώνως τὴν ἐπομένην εὐχήν·)*

Δέσποτα Κύριε, ὁ Θεὸς ἡμῶν, ὁ καταστήσας
ἐν οὐρανοῖς τάγματα καὶ στρατιὰς ἀγγέλων
καὶ ἀρχαγγέλων, εἰς λειτουργίαν τῆς σῆς
δόξης, ποίησον σὺν τῇ εἰσόδῳ ἡμῶν εἴσοδον
ἁγίων ἀγγέλων γενέσθαι, συλλειτουργούντων
ἡμῖν καὶ συνδοξολογούντων τὴν σὴν ἀγαθότητα.
῞Οτι πρέπει σοι πᾶσα δόξα, τιμὴ καὶ προσκύνησις, τῷ Πατρὶ καὶ τῷ Υἱῷ καὶ τῷ ῾Αγίῳ
Πνεύματι, νῦν καὶ ἀεὶ καὶ εἰς τοὺς αἰῶνας τῶν
αἰώνων. ᾽Αμήν.

now the petitions of Your servants for our benefit, giving us the knowledge of Your truth in this world, and granting us eternal life in the world to come.

Priest: For You are a good and loving God, and to You we give glory, to the Father and the Son and the Holy Spirit, now and forever and to the ages of ages.

People: **Amen.**

THE THIRD ANTIPHON

(The designated verses of the Psalms are sung with the Apolytikion.)

THE ENTRANCE

(While the Apolytikion is sung, the priest carrying the holy Gospel Book comes in procession before the Beautiful Gate of the Iconostasis offering in a low voice the following prayer:)

Master and Lord our God, You have established in heaven the orders and hosts of angels and archangels to minister to Your glory. Grant that the holy angels may enter with us that together we may serve and glorify Your goodness. For to You belong all glory, honor, and worship to the Father and the Son and the Holy Spirit, now and forever and to the ages of ages. Amen.

(Ὁ Ἱερεὺς εὐλογῶν τὴν Εἴσοδον λέγει χαμη-
λοφώνως·) Εὐλογημένη ἡ εἴσοδος τῶν ἁγίων
σου πάντοτε, νῦν καὶ ἀεὶ καὶ εἰς τοὺς αἰῶνας
τῶν αἰώνων. Ἀμήν.

(Μετὰ ὑψώνει τὸ Ἱερὸν Εὐαγγέλιον καὶ λέγει·)

*Ἱερεύς: Σοφία. Ὀρθοί.

Λαός: Δεῦτε προσκυνήσωμεν καὶ προσπέσω-
μεν Χριστῷ. Σῶσον ἡμᾶς Υἱὲ Θεοῦ, ὁ ἀναστὰς ἐκ νεκρῶν,[1] ψάλλοντάς σοι· Ἀλληλούϊα.

(Ὁ Ἱερεὺς εἰσέρχεται εἰς τὸ Ἱερὸν Βῆμα. Ἐπα-
ναλαμβάνονται τὰ Ἀπολυτίκια τῆς ἡμέρας μετὰ
τοῦ Τροπαρίου τοῦ Ἁγίου τοῦ Ναοῦ καὶ τὸ
Κοντάκιον.)

Ο ΤΡΙΣΑΓΙΟΣ ΥΜΝΟΣ

*Ἱερεύς: Τοῦ Κυρίου δεηθῶμεν.

Λαός: Κύριε, ἐλέησον.

Ἱερεύς (χαμηλοφώνως): Ὁ Θεὸς ὁ ἅγιος, ὁ ἐν
ἁγίοις ἀναπαυόμενος, ὁ τρισαγίῳ φωνῇ ὑπὸ
τῶν Σεραφεὶμ ἀνυμνούμενος καὶ ὑπὸ τῶν Χερουβεὶμ δοξολογούμενος καὶ ὑπὸ πάσης ἐπου-

---

[1] Εἰς τὰς καθημερινὰς ψάλλεται τό: «ὁ ἐν ἁγίοις
θαυμαστός». Αἱ δεσποτικαὶ ἑορταὶ ἔχουν ἴδιον
Εἰσοδικόν.

(*The priest blesses the entrance saying in a low voice:*) Blessed is the entrance of Your saints always, now and forever and to the ages of ages. Amen.

(*He then raises the holy Gospel Book and says:*)

Priest: Wisdom. Let us be attentive.

People: **Come, let us worship and bow before Christ. Save us, O Son of God (who rose from the dead),**[1] **to You we sing: Alleluia.**

(*The priest enters the sanctuary. The Apolytikion is repeated and the Troparion of the church and the Kontakion of the day are sung.*)

THE TRISAGION HYMN

Priest: Let us pray to the Lord.

People: **Lord, have mercy.**

Priest (in a low voice): Holy God, You dwell among Your saints. You are praised by the Seraphim with the thrice holy hymn and glorified by the Cherubim and worshiped by all the

---

[1] *On weekdays we sing: ("who are wondrous among Your saints"), while the Feasts of the Lord have their own Entrance Hymns."*

ρανίου δυνάμεως προσκυνούμενος· ὁ ἐκ τοῦ
μὴ ὄντος εἰς τὸ εἶναι παραγαγὼν τὰ σύμπαντα·
ὁ κτίσας τὸν ἄνθρωπον κατ᾽ εἰκόνα σὴν καὶ
ὁμοίωσιν καὶ παντί σου χαρίσματι κατακο-
σμήσας· ὁ διδοὺς αἰτοῦντι σοφίαν καὶ σύνεσιν
καὶ μὴ παρορῶν ἁμαρτάνοντα, ἀλλὰ θέμενος
ἐπὶ σωτηρίᾳ μετάνοιαν· ὁ καταξιώσας ἡμᾶς,
τοὺς ταπεινοὺς καὶ ἀναξίους δούλους σου καὶ
ἐν τῇ ὥρᾳ ταύτῃ στῆναι κατενώπιον τῆς δόξης
τοῦ ἁγίου σου θυσιαστηρίου καὶ τὴν ὀφειλομέ-
νην σοι προσκύνησιν καὶ δοξολογίαν προσά-
γειν· αὐτός Δέσποτα, πρόσδεξαι καὶ ἐκ στόμα-
τος ἡμῶν τῶν ἁμαρτωλῶν τὸν τρισάγιον ὕμνον
καὶ ἐπίσκεψαι ἡμᾶς ἐν τῇ χρηστότητί σου.
Συγχώρησον ἡμῖν πᾶν πλημμέλημα ἑκούσιόν
τε καὶ ἀκούσιον· ἁγίασον ἡμῶν τὰς ψυχὰς καὶ
τὰ σώματα· καὶ δὸς ἡμῖν ἐν ὁσιότητι λατρεύειν
σοι πάσας τὰς ἡμέρας τῆς ζωῆς ἡμῶν· πρεσβείαις τῆς ἁγίας Θεοτόκου καὶ πάντων τῶν
ἁγίων, τῶν ἀπ᾽ αἰῶνός σοι εὐαρεστησάντων.

Ἱερεύς: Ὅτι ἅγιος εἶ ὁ Θεὸς ἡμῶν, καὶ σοὶ
τὴν δόξαν ἀναπέμπομεν, τῷ Πατρὶ καὶ τῷ
Υἱῷ καὶ τῷ Ἁγίῳ Πνεύματι, νῦν καὶ ἀεὶ . . .
*καὶ εἰς τοὺς αἰῶνας τῶν αἰώνων.

Λαός: **Ἀμήν. Ἅγιος ὁ Θεός, ἅγιος ἰσχυρός,
ἅγιος ἀθάνατος, ἐλέησον ἡμᾶς** (3).

**Δόξα Πατρὶ καὶ Υἱῷ καὶ Ἁγίῳ Πνεύματι καὶ
νῦν καὶ ἀεὶ καὶ εἰς τοὺς αἰῶνας τῶν αἰώνων.**

Ἀμήν. Ἅγιος ἀθάνατος, ἐλέησον ἡμᾶς.

heavenly powers. You have brought all things out of nothing into being. You have created man and woman in Your image and likeness and adorned them with all the gifts of Your grace. You give wisdom and understanding to the supplicant and do not overlook the sinner but have established repentance as the way of salvation. You have enabled us, Your lowly and unworthy servants, to stand at this hour before the glory of Your holy altar and to offer to You due worship and praise. Master, accept the thrice holy hymn also from the lips of us sinners and visit us in Your goodness. Forgive our voluntary and involuntary transgressions, sanctify our souls and bodies, and grant that we may worship and serve You in holiness all the days of our lives, by the intercessions of the holy Theotokos and of all the saints who have pleased You throughout the ages.

Priest: For You are holy, our God, and to You we give glory, to the Father and the Son and the Holy Spirit, now and forever . . . *and to the ages of ages.

People: **Amen. Holy God, Holy Mighty, Holy Immortal, have mercy on us** (*3*).

Glory to the Father and the Son and the Holy Spirit, now and forever and to the ages of ages.

Amen. Holy Immortal, have mercy on us.

*Ἱερεύς: Δύναμις.

(Ὁ Ἱερεύς στρέφων πρὸς τὴν Πρόθεσιν, λέγει χαμηλοφώνως·) Εὐλογημένος ὁ ἐρχόμενος ἐν ὀνόματι Κυρίου. Εὐλογημένος εἶ ὁ ἐπὶ θρόνου δόξης τῆς βασιλείας σου, ὁ καθήμενος ἐπὶ τῶν Χερουβείμ, πάντοτε· νῦν καὶ ἀεὶ καὶ εἰς τοὺς αἰῶνας τῶν αἰώνων. Ἀμήν.

Λαός: Ἅγιος ὁ Θεός, ἅγιος ἰσχυρός, ἅγιος ἀθάνατος, ἐλέησον ἡμᾶς.

ΤΑ ΑΝΑΓΝΩΣΜΑΤΑ

Ο ΑΠΟΣΤΟΛΟΣ

*Ἱερεύς: Πρόσχωμεν.

(Ὁ Ἀναγνώστης ἐκφωνεῖ τοὺς στίχους τῶν Ψαλμῶν.)

*Ἱερεύς: Σοφία.

Ἀναγνώστης: Πράξεων τῶν Ἀποστόλων (ἢ Πρὸς. . .Ἐπιστολῆς Παύλου ἢ Καθολικῆς Ἐπιστολῆς. . .) τὸ ἀνάγνωσμα.

*Ἱερεύς: Πρόσχωμεν.

(Ὁ Ἀναγνώστης ἀναγινώσκει τὴν τεταγμένην ἀποστολικὴν περικοπήν.)

Ἱερεύς: Εἰρήνη σοι.

Λαός: Ἀλληλούϊα· Ἀλληλούϊα· Ἀλληλούϊα.

Priest: **Again, fervently.**

(*The priest, turning towards the Prothesis, says in a low voice:*) **Blessed is He who comes in the name of the Lord. Blessed are You on the throne of glory of Your kingdom, seated upon the Cherubim, now and forever and to the ages of ages. Amen.**

People: **Holy God, Holy Mighty, Holy Immortal, have mercy on us.**

THE READINGS

THE EPISTLE

Priest: **Let us be attentive.**

(*The Reader reads the verses from the Psalms.*)

Priest: **Wisdom.**

Reader: **The reading is from** (*the name of the book of the New Testament from which the Apostolic reading is taken*).

Priest: **Let us be attentive.**

(*The Reader reads the designated Apostolic pericope.*)

Priest: **Peace be with you.**

People: **Alleluia. Alleluia. Alleluia.**

Ἰερεύς: Ἔλλαμψον ἐν ταῖς καρδίαις ἡμῶν, φιλάνθρωπε Δέσποτα, τὸ τῆς σῆς θεογνωσίας ἀκήρατον φῶς καὶ τοὺς τῆς διανοίας ἡμῶν ὀφθαλμοὺς διάνοιξον εἰς τὴν τῶν εὐαγγελικῶν σου κηρυγμάτων κατανόησιν. Ἔνθες ἡμῖν καὶ τὸν τῶν μακαρίων σου ἐντολῶν φόβον, ἵνα, τὰς σαρκικὰς ἐπιθυμίας πάσας καταπατήσαντες, πνευματικὴν πολιτείαν μετέλθωμεν, πάντα τὰ πρὸς εὐαρέστησιν τὴν σὴν καὶ φρονοῦντες καὶ πράττοντες. Σὺ γὰρ εἶ ὁ φωτισμὸς τῶν ψυχῶν καὶ τῶν σωμάτων ἡμῶν, Χριστὲ ὁ Θεός, καὶ σοὶ τὴν δόξαν ἀναπέμπομεν σὺν τῷ ἀνάρχῳ σου Πατρὶ καὶ τῷ παναγίῳ καὶ ἀγαθῷ καὶ ζωοποιῷ σου Πνεύματι, νῦν καὶ ἀεὶ καὶ εἰς τοὺς αἰῶνας τῶν αἰώνων. Ἀμήν.

ΤΟ ΘΕΙΟΝ ΕΥΑΓΓΕΛΙΟΝ

Ἰερεύς: Σοφία. Ὀρθοί. Ἀκούσωμεν τοῦ ἁγίου Εὐαγγελίου. Εἰρήνη πᾶσι.

Λαός: **Καὶ τῷ πνεύματί σου.**

* Ἰερεύς: Ἐκ τοῦ κατὰ (*Ὄνομα*) ἁγίου Εὐαγγελίου τὸ Ἀνάγνωσμα. Πρόσχωμεν.

Λαός: **Δόξα σοι, Κύριε, δόξα σοι.**

(**Ὁ Ἰερεὺς ἀναγινώσκει τὴν τεταγμένην περικοπὴν τοῦ ἁγίου Εὐαγγελίου.*)

Λαός: **Δόξα σοι, Κύριε, δόξα σοι.**

Priest (in a low voice): Shine within our hearts, loving Master, the pure light of Your divine knowledge and open the eyes of our minds that we may comprehend the message of your Gospel. Instill in us also reverence for Your blessed commandments, so that having conquered sinful desires, we may pursue a spiritual life, thinking and doing all those things that are pleasing to You. For You, Christ our God, are the light of our souls and bodies, and to You we give glory together with Your Father who is without beginning and Your all holy, good, and life giving Spirit, now and forever and to the ages of ages. Amen.

THE GOSPEL

Priest: Wisdom. Arise. Let us hear the holy Gospel. Peace be with all.

People: **And with your spirit.**

*Priest: The reading is from the holy Gospel according to (*Name*). Let us be attentive.

People: **Glory to You, O Lord, glory to You.**

(**The Priest reads the designated pericope of the holy Gospel.*)

People: **Glory to You, O Lord, glory to You.**

ΤΟ ΘΕΙΟΝ ΚΗΡΥΓΜΑ

(Μετὰ τὰ ἀναγνώσματα εἴθισται ἡ ἐκφώνησις τοῦ θείου λόγου.)

ΕΥΧΗ ΤΩΝ ΠΙΣΤΩΝ

Ἱερεύς (χαμηλοφώνως): **Πάλιν καὶ πολλάκις σοὶ προσπίπτομεν καὶ σοῦ δεόμεθα, ἀγαθὲ καὶ φιλάνθρωπε, ὅπως, ἐπιβλέψας ἐπὶ τὴν δέησιν ἡμῶν, καθαρίσῃς ἡμῶν τὰς ψυχὰς καὶ τὰ σώματα ἀπὸ παντὸς μολυσμοῦ σαρκὸς καὶ πνεύματος· καὶ δῴης ἡμῖν ἀνένοχον καὶ ἀκατάκριτον τὴν παράστασιν τοῦ ἁγίου σου θυσιαστηρίου. Χάρισαι δέ, ὁ Θεός, καὶ τοῖς συνευχομένοις ἡμῖν προκοπὴν βίου καὶ πίστεως καὶ συνέσεως πνευματικῆς· δὸς αὐτοῖς πάντοτε μετὰ φόβου καὶ ἀγάπης λατρεύειν σοι, ἀνενόχως καὶ ἀκατακρίτως μετέχειν τῶν ἁγίων σου μυστηρίων, καὶ τῆς ἐπουρανίου σου βασιλείας ἀξιωθῆναι.**

Ἱερεύς: **Ὅπως ὑπὸ τοῦ κράτους σου πάντοτε φυλαττόμενοι, σοὶ δόξαν ἀναπέμπωμεν, τῷ Πατρὶ καὶ τῷ Υἱῷ καὶ τῷ Ἁγίῳ Πνεύματι, νῦν καὶ ἀεὶ καὶ εἰς τοὺς αἰῶνας τῶν αἰώνων.**

Λαός: **Ἀμήν.**

Η ΜΕΓΑΛΗ ΕΙΣΟΔΟΣ

Λαός: **Οἱ τὰ Χερουβεὶμ μυστικῶς εἰκονίζοντες καὶ τῇ ζωοποιῷ Τριάδι τὸν τρισάγιον ὕμνον προσάδοντες, πᾶσαν τὴν βιοτικὴν ἀποθώμεθα**

THE HOMILY

(Following the readings, it is customary for the priest to proclaim the Gospel.)

PRAYER OF THE FAITHFUL

Priest (in a low voice): **Again, we bow before You and pray to You, O good and loving God. Hear our supplication: cleanse our souls and bodies from every defilement of flesh and spirit, and grant that we may stand before Your holy altar without blame or condemnation. Grant also, O God, progress in life, faith, and spiritual discernment to the faithful who pray with us, so that they may always worship You with reverence and love, partake of Your Holy Mysteries without blame or condemnation, and become worthy of Your heavenly kingdom.**

Priest: **And grant that always guarded by Your power we may give glory to You, the Father and the Son and the Holy Spirit, now and forever and to the ages of ages.**

People: **Amen.**

THE GREAT ENTRANCE

People: **We who mystically represent the Cherubim sing the thrice holy hymn to the life giving Trinity. Let us set aside all the cares of**

μέριμναν. Ὡς τὸν βασιλέα τῶν ὅλων ὑποδεξόμενοι. . .

(*Ψαλλομένου τοῦ Χερουβικοῦ ὁ Ἱερεὺς λέγει χαμηλοφώνως·*) Οὐδεὶς ἄξιος τῶν συνδεδεμένων ταῖς σαρκικαῖς ἐπιθυμίαις καὶ ἡδοναῖς προσέρχεσθαι ἢ προσεγγίζειν ἢ λειτουργεῖν σοι, βασιλεῦ τῆς δόξης. Τὸ γὰρ διακονεῖν σοι μέγα καὶ φοβερὸν καὶ αὐταῖς ταῖς ἐπουρανίαις δυνάμεσιν. Ἀλλ᾽ ὅμως, διὰ τὴν ἄφατον καὶ ἀμέτρητόν σου φιλανθρωπίαν, ἀτρέπτως καὶ ἀναλλοιώτως γέγονας ἄνθρωπος καὶ ἀρχιερεὺς ἡμῶν ἐχρημάτισας καὶ τῆς λειτουργικῆς ταύτης καὶ ἀναιμάκτου θυσίας τὴν ἱερουργίαν παρέδωκας ἡμῖν, ὡς δεσπότης τῶν ἁπάντων. Σὺ γὰρ μόνος, Κύριε ὁ Θεὸς ἡμῶν, δεσπόζεις τῶν ἐπουρανίων καὶ τῶν ἐπιγείων, ὁ ἐπὶ θρόνου χερουβικοῦ ἐποχούμενος, ὁ τῶν Σεραφεὶμ Κύριος καὶ βασιλεὺς τοῦ Ἰσραήλ, ὁ μόνος ἅγιος καὶ ἐν ἁγίοις ἀναπαυόμενος. Σὲ τοίνυν δυσωπῶ τὸν μόνον ἀγαθὸν καὶ εὐήκοον· ἐπίβλεψον ἐπ᾽ ἐμὲ τὸν ἁμαρτωλὸν καὶ ἀχρεῖον δοῦλόν σου καὶ καθάρισόν μου τὴν ψυχὴν καὶ τὴν καρδίαν ἀπὸ συνειδήσεως πονηρᾶς· καὶ ἱκάνωσόν με τῇ δυνάμει τοῦ Ἁγίου σου Πνεύματος, ἐνδεδυμένον τὴν τῆς ἱερατείας χάριν, παραστῆναι τῇ ἁγίᾳ σου ταύτῃ τραπέζῃ καὶ ἱερουργῆσαι τὸ ἅγιον καὶ ἄχραντόν σου Σῶμα καὶ τὸ τίμιον Αἷμα. Σοὶ γὰρ προσέρχομαι, κλίνας τὸν ἐμαυτοῦ αὐχένα, καὶ δέομαί σου· μὴ ἀποστρέψῃς τὸ πρόσωπόν σου ἀπ᾽ ἐμοῦ, μηδὲ ἀποδοκιμάσῃς με ἐκ παίδων σου, ἀλλ᾽ ἀξίωσον

life that we may receive the King of all . . .

(*While the Cherubic Hymn is being sung, the Priest prays in a low voice:*) No one bound by worldly desires and pleasures is worthy to approach, draw near or minister to You, the King of glory. To serve You is great and awesome even for the heavenly powers. But because of Your ineffable and immeasurable love for us, You became man without alteration or change. You have served as our High Priest, and as Lord of all, and have entrusted to us the celebration of this liturgical sacrifice without the shedding of blood. For You alone, Lord our God, rule over all things in heaven and on earth. You are seated on the throne of the Cherubim, the Lord of the Seraphim and the King of Israel. You alone are holy and dwell among Your saints. You alone are good and ready to hear. Therefore, I implore you, look upon me, Your sinful and unworthy servant, and cleanse my soul and heart from evil consciousness. Enable me by the power of Your Holy Spirit so that, vested with the grace of priesthood, I may stand before Your holy Table and celebrate the mystery of Your holy and pure Body and Your precious Blood. To you I come with bowed head and pray: do not turn Your face away from me or reject me from among Your children, but make me, Your sinful and un-

προσενεχθῆναί σοι ὑπ' ἐμοῦ τοῦ ἁμαρτωλοῦ καὶ ἀναξίου δούλου σου τὰ δῶρα ταῦτα. Σὺ γὰρ εἶ ὁ προσφέρων καὶ προσφερόμενος καὶ προσδεχόμενος καὶ διαδιδόμενος, Χριστὲ ὁ Θεὸς ἡμῶν, καὶ σοὶ τὴν δόξαν ἀναπέμπομεν, σὺν τῷ ἀνάρχῳ σου Πατρὶ καὶ τῷ παναγίῳ καὶ ἀγαθῷ καὶ ζωοποιῷ σου Πνεύματι, νῦν καὶ ἀεὶ καὶ εἰς τοὺς αἰῶνας τῶν αἰώνων. Ἀμήν.

(Ὁ Ἱερεὺς θυμιᾷ καὶ λέγει χαμηλοφώνως τὸν Χερουβικὸν Ὕμνον, τὸ Ἀνάστασιν Χριστοῦ θεασάμενοι, εἰς τὰς Κυριακάς, καὶ τὸν 50ον Ψαλμόν. Μετὰ γίνεται ἡ Μεγάλη Εἴσοδος).

*Ἱερεύς: Πάντων ὑμῶν μνησθείη Κύριος ὁ Θεὸς ἐν τῇ βασιλείᾳ αὐτοῦ πάντοτε, νῦν καὶ ἀεὶ καὶ εἰς τοὺς αἰῶνας τῶν αἰώνων.

Λαός: Ἀμήν.

(Ὁ Ἱερεὺς εἰσέρχεται εἰς τὸ Ἱερὸν Βῆμα, ὁ δὲ λαὸς ψάλλει τὸ τέλος τοῦ Χερουβικοῦ.)

Λαός: Ταῖς ἀγγελικαῖς ἀοράτως δορυφορούμενον τάξεσιν. Ἀλληλούϊα. Ἀλληλούϊα. Ἀλληλούϊα.

(Ἀποτιθεὶς τὰ τίμια δῶρα ἐπὶ τῆς ἁγίας Τραπέζης, ὁ Ἱερεὺς λέγει·)

ΤΑ ΠΛΗΡΩΤΙΚΑ

*Ἱερεύς: Πληρώσωμεν τὴν δέησιν ἡμῶν τῷ Κυρίῳ.

worthy servant, worthy to offer to You these gifts. For You, Christ our God, are the Offerer and the Offered, the One who receives and is distributed, and to You we give glory, together with Your eternal Father and Your holy, good and life giving Spirit, now and forever and to the ages of ages. Amen.

(*The Priest censes and recites in a low voice the* **"Cherubic Hymn," "Having Beheld Christ's Resurrection"** *(on Sundays), and the* **50th Psalm**. *Then the Great Entrance takes place.*)

Priest: May the Lord God remember all of you in His kingdom, now and forever and to the ages of ages.

People: **Amen.**

(*The priest enters the sanctuary, while the people sing the end of the Cherubic Hymn.*)

People: . . . **invisibly escorted by the angelic hosts. Alleluia. Alleluia. Alleluia.**

(*After placing the holy gifts on the holy Table, the priest says:*)

THE PETITIONS

Priest: Let us complete our prayer to the Lord.

Λαός: **Κύριε, ἐλέησον.**

Ἱερεύς: Ὑπὲρ τῶν προτεθέντων τιμίων δώρων, τοῦ Κυρίου δεηθῶμεν.

Λαός: **Κύριε, ἐλέησον.**

Ἱερεύς: Ὑπὲρ τοῦ ἁγίου οἴκου τούτου καὶ τῶν μετὰ πίστεως, εὐλαβείας καὶ φόβου Θεοῦ εἰσιόντων ἐν αὐτῷ, τοῦ Κυρίου δεηθῶμεν.

Λαός: **Κύριε, ἐλέησον.**

Ἱερεύς: Ὑπὲρ τοῦ ῥυσθῆναι ἡμᾶς ἀπὸ πάσης θλίψεως, ὀργῆς, κινδύνου καὶ ἀνάγκης, τοῦ Κυρίου δεηθῶμεν.

Λαός: **Κύριε, ἐλέησον.**

Ἱερεύς: Ἀντιλαβοῦ, σῶσον, ἐλέησον καὶ διαφύλαξον ἡμᾶς, ὁ Θεός, τῇ σῇ χάριτι.

Λαός: **Κύριε, ἐλέησον.**

Ἱερεύς: Τὴν ἡμέραν πᾶσαν τελείαν, ἁγίαν, εἰρηνικὴν καὶ ἀναμάρτητον, παρὰ τοῦ Κυρίου αἰτησώμεθα.

Λαός: **Παράσχου, Κύριε.**

Ἱερεύς: Ἄγγελον εἰρήνης, πιστὸν ὁδηγόν, φύλακα τῶν ψυχῶν καὶ τῶν σωμάτων ἡμῶν, παρὰ τοῦ Κυρίου αἰτησώμεθα.

People: **Lord, have mercy.**

*Priest: For the precious gifts here presented, let us pray to the Lord.

People: **Lord, have mercy.**

*Priest: For this holy house and for those who enter it with faith, reverence, and the fear of God, let us pray to the Lord.

People: **Lord, have mercy.**

*Priest: For our deliverance from all affliction, wrath, danger, and distress, let us pray to the Lord.

People: **Lord, have mercy.**

*Priest: Help us, save us, have mercy upon us, and protect us, O God, by Your grace.

People: **Lord, have mercy.**

*Priest: For a perfect, holy, peaceful, and sinless day, let us ask the Lord.

People: **Grant this, O Lord.**

*Priest: For an angel of peace, a faithful guide, a guardian of our souls and bodies, let us ask the Lord.

Λαὸς: **Παράσχου, Κύριε.**

*Ἱερεύς: Συγγνώμην καὶ ἄφεσιν τῶν ἁμαρτιῶν καὶ τῶν πλημμελημάτων ἡμῶν, παρὰ τοῦ Κυρίου αἰτησώμεθα.

Λαὸς: **Παράσχου, Κύριε.**

*Ἱερεύς: Τὰ καλὰ καὶ συμφέροντα ταῖς ψυχαῖς ἡμῶν καὶ εἰρήνην τῷ κόσμῳ, παρὰ τοῦ Κυρίου αἰτησώμεθα.

Λαὸς: **Παράσχου, Κύριε.**

*Ἱερεύς: Τὸν ὑπόλοιπον χρόνον τῆς ζωῆς ἡμῶν ἐν εἰρήνῃ καὶ μετανοίᾳ ἐκτελέσαι, παρὰ τοῦ Κυρίου αἰτησώμεθα.

Λαὸς: **Παράσχου, Κύριε.**

*Ἱερεύς: Χριστιανὰ τὰ τέλη τῆς ζωῆς ἡμῶν, ἀνώδυνα, ἀνεπαίσχυντα, εἰρηνικὰ καὶ καλὴν ἀπολογίαν τὴν ἐπὶ τοῦ φοβεροῦ βήματος τοῦ Χριστοῦ αἰτησώμεθα.

Λαὸς: **Παράσχου, Κύριε.**

*Ἱερεύς: Τῆς παναγίας, ἀχράντου, ὑπερευλογημένης, ἐνδόξου, δεσποίνης ἡμῶν Θεοτόκου καὶ ἀειπαρθένου Μαρίας, μετὰ πάντων τῶν ἁγίων μνημονεύσαντες, ἑαυτοὺς καὶ ἀλλήλους καὶ πᾶσαν τὴν ζωὴν ἡμῶν Χριστῷ τῷ Θεῷ παραθώμεθα.

People: **Grant this, O Lord.**

*Priest: For forgiveness and remission of our sins and transgressions, let us ask the Lord.

People: **Grant this, O Lord.**

*Priest: For all that is good and beneficial to our souls, and for peace in the world, let us ask the Lord.

People: **Grant this, O Lord.**

*Priest: For the completion of our lives in peace and repentance, let us ask the Lord.

People: **Grant this, O Lord.**

*Priest: For a Christian end to our lives, peaceful, without shame and suffering, and for a good account before the awesome judgment seat of Christ, let us ask the Lord.

People: **Grant this, O Lord.**

*Priest: Remembering our most holy, pure, blessed, and glorious Lady, the Theotokos and ever virgin Mary, with all the saints, let us commit ourselves and one another and our whole life to Christ our God.

Λαός: **Σοί, Κύριε.**

Η ΕΥΧΗ ΤΗΣ ΠΡΟΣΚΟΜΙΔΗΣ

Ἱερεύς (χαμηλοφώνως): Κύριε ὁ Θεὸς ὁ παντοτοκράτωρ, ὁ μόνος ἅγιος, ὁ δεχόμενος θυσίαν αἰνέσεως παρὰ τῶν ἐπικαλουμένων σε ἐν ὅλῃ καρδίᾳ, πρόσδεξαι καὶ ἡμῶν τῶν ἁμαρτωλῶν τὴν δέησιν καὶ προσάγαγε τῷ ἁγίῳ σου θυσιαστηρίῳ· καὶ ἱκάνωσον ἡμᾶς προσενεγκεῖν σοι δῶρά τε καὶ θυσίας πνευματικὰς ὑπὲρ τῶν ἡμετέρων ἁμαρτημάτων καὶ τῶν τοῦ λαοῦ ἀγνοημάτων. Καὶ καταξίωσον ἡμᾶς, εὑρεῖν χάριν ἐνώπιόν σου, τοῦ γενέσθαι σοι εὐπρόσδεκτον τὴν θυσίαν ἡμῶν καὶ ἐπισκηνῶσαι τὸ Πνεῦμα τῆς χάριτός σου τὸ ἀγαθὸν ἐφ᾽ ἡμᾶς καὶ ἐπὶ τὰ προκείμενα δῶρα ταῦτα, καὶ ἐπὶ πάντα τὸν λαόν σου.

Ἱερεύς: Διὰ τῶν οἰκτιρμῶν τοῦ μονογενοῦς σου Υἱοῦ, μεθ᾽ οὗ εὐλογητὸς εἶ, σὺν τῷ παναγίῳ καὶ ἀγαθῷ καὶ ζωοποιῷ σου Πνεύματι, νῦν καὶ ἀεὶ καὶ εἰς τοὺς αἰῶνας τῶν αἰώνων.

Λαός: **Ἀμήν.**

Ἱερεύς: Εἰρήνη πᾶσι.

Λαός: **Καὶ τῷ πνεύματί σου.**

* *Ἱερεύς:* Ἀγαπήσωμεν ἀλλήλους, ἵνα ἐν ὁμονοίᾳ ὁμολογήσωμεν.

(*Ὁ Ἱερεὺς ἀσπαζόμενος τὰ τίμια δῶρα λέγει·*)
Ἀγαπήσω σε, Κύριε, ἡ ἰσχύς μου. Κύριος στερέωμά μου, καὶ καταφυγή μου καὶ ῥύστης μου.

People: **To You, O Lord.**

THE PRAYER OF THE PROSKOMIDE

Priest (in a low voice): Lord, God Almighty, You alone are holy. You accept a sacrifice of praise from those who call upon You with their whole heart. Receive also the prayer of us sinners and let it reach Your holy altar. Enable us to bring before You gifts and spiritual sacrifices for our sins and for the transgressions of the people. Make us worthy to find grace in Your presence so that our sacrifice may be pleasing to You and that Your good and gracious Spirit may abide with us, with the gifts here presented, and with all Your people.

Priest: Through the mercies of Your only begotten Son with whom You are blessed, together with Your all holy, good, and life giving Spirit, now and forever and to the ages of ages.

People: **Amen.**

Priest: Peace be with all.

People: **And with your spirit.**

* *Priest:* Let us love one another that with one mind we may confess:

(*The Priest kisses the holy Gifts saying:*) I love You, Lord, my strength. The Lord is my rock, and my fortress, and my deliverer.

(Εἰς τὸ σημεῖον αὐτὸ εἴθισται νὰ γίνεται ὁ ἀσπασμὸς τῆς εἰρήνης.)

Λαός: **Πατέρα, Υἱὸν καὶ Ἅγιον Πνεῦμα, Τριάδα ὁμοούσιον καὶ ἀχώριστον.**

* Ἱερεύς: Τὰς θύρας, τὰς θύρας· ἐν σοφίᾳ πρόσχωμεν.

ΣΥΜΒΟΛΟΝ ΤΗΣ ΠΙΣΤΕΩΣ

Λαός: **Πιστεύω εἰς ἕνα Θεόν, Πατέρα, παντοκράτορα, ποιητὴν οὐρανοῦ καὶ γῆς, ὁρατῶν τε πάντων καὶ ἀοράτων.**

Καὶ εἰς ἕνα Κύριον, Ἰησοῦν Χριστόν, τὸν Υἱὸν τοῦ Θεοῦ τὸν μονογενῆ, τὸν ἐκ τοῦ Πατρὸς γεννηθέντα πρὸ πάντων τῶν αἰώνων. Φῶς ἐκ φωτός, Θεὸν ἀληθινὸν ἐκ Θεοῦ ἀληθινοῦ γεννηθέντα, οὐ ποιηθέντα, ὁμοούσιον τῷ Πατρί, δι' οὗ τὰ πάντα ἐγένετο.

Τὸν δι' ἡμᾶς τοὺς ἀνθρώπους καὶ διὰ τὴν ἡμετέραν σωτηρίαν κατελθόντα ἐκ τῶν οὐρανῶν καὶ σαρκωθέντα ἐκ Πνεύματος Ἁγίου καὶ Μαρίας τῆς Παρθένου καὶ ἐνανθρωπήσαντα.

Σταυρωθέντα τε ὑπὲρ ἡμῶν ἐπὶ Ποντίου Πιλάτου καὶ παθόντα καὶ ταφέντα.

Καὶ ἀναστάντα τῇ τρίτῃ ἡμέρᾳ κατὰ τὰς Γραφάς.

Καὶ ἀνελθόντα εἰς τοὺς οὐρανοὺς καὶ καθεζόμενον ἐκ δεξιῶν τοῦ Πατρός.

Καὶ πάλιν ἐρχόμενον μετὰ δόξης κρῖναι

(*At this time it is customary for the kiss of peace to be exchanged.*)

People: **Father, Son, and Holy Spirit, Trinity one in essence and inseparable.**

*Priest: Guard the doors. Wisdom. Let us be attentive.

THE CREED

People: **I believe in one God, the Father, the Almighty, Creator of heaven and earth, and of all things visible and invisible.**

And in one Lord, Jesus Christ, the only begotten Son of God, begotten of the Father before all ages. Light of Light, true God of true God, begotten, not created, of one essence with the Father, through whom all things were made.

For us and for our salvation, He came down from heaven and was incarnate by the Holy Spirit and the Virgin Mary and became man.

He was crucified for us under Pontius Pilate, and He suffered and was buried.

On the third day He rose according to the Scriptures.

He ascended into heaven and is seated at the right hand of the Father.

He will come again in glory to judge the living

ζῶντας καὶ νεκρούς, οὗ τῆς βασιλείας οὐκ ἔσται τέλος.

Καὶ εἰς τὸ Πνεῦμα τὸ Ἅγιον, τὸ Κύριον, τὸ ζωοποιόν, τὸ ἐκ τοῦ Πατρὸς ἐκπορευόμενον, τὸ σὺν Πατρὶ καὶ Υἱῷ συμπροσκυνούμενον καὶ συνδοξαζόμενον, τὸ λαλῆσαν διὰ τῶν Προφητῶν.

Εἰς μίαν, ἁγίαν, καθολικὴν καὶ ἀποστολικὴν Ἐκκλησίαν.

Ὁμολογῶ ἓν βάπτισμα εἰς ἄφεσιν ἁμαρτιῶν.

Προσδοκῶ ἀνάστασιν νεκρῶν.

Καὶ ζωὴν τοῦ μέλλοντος αἰῶνος. Ἀμήν.

Η ΑΓΙΑ ΑΝΑΦΟΡΑ

Ἱερεύς: Στῶμεν καλῶς· στῶμεν μετὰ φόβου· πρόσχωμεν· τὴν ἁγίαν ἀναφορὰν ἐν εἰρήνῃ προσφέρειν.

Λαός: Ἔλεον εἰρήνης, θυσίαν αἰνέσεως.

Ἱερεύς: Ἡ χάρις τοῦ Κυρίου ἡμῶν Ἰησοῦ Χριστοῦ καὶ ἡ ἀγάπη τοῦ Θεοῦ καὶ Πατρὸς καὶ ἡ κοινωνία τοῦ ἁγίου Πνεύματος, εἴη μετὰ πάντων ὑμῶν.

Λαός: Καὶ μετὰ τοῦ πνεύματός σου.

Ἱερεύς: Ἄνω σχῶμεν τὰς καρδίας.

Λαός: Ἔχομεν πρὸς τὸν Κύριον.

Ἱερεύς: Εὐχαριστήσωμεν τῷ Κυρίῳ.

and the dead. His kingdom will have no end.

And in the Holy Spirit, the Lord, the Giver of Life, who proceeds from the Father, who together with the Father and the Son is worshiped and glorified, who spoke through the prophets.

In one, holy, catholic, and apostolic Church.

I acknowledge one baptism for the forgiveness of sins.

I expect the resurrection of the dead.

And the life of the age to come. Amen.

THE HOLY ANAPHORA

Priest: Let us stand well. Let us stand in awe. Let us be attentive, that we may present the holy offering in peace.

People: **Mercy and peace, a sacrifice of praise.**

Priest: The grace of our Lord Jesus Christ, and the love of God the Father, and the communion of the Holy Spirit, be with all of you.

People: **And with your spirit.**

Priest: Let us lift up our hearts.

People: **We lift them up to the Lord.**

Priest: Let us give thanks to the Lord.

Λαός: **Ἄξιον καὶ δίκαιον.**

Ἱερεύς (χαμηλοφώνως): Ἄξιον καὶ δίκαιον σὲ ὑμνεῖν, σὲ εὐλογεῖν, σὲ αἰνεῖν, σοὶ εὐχαριστεῖν, σὲ προσκυνεῖν ἐν παντὶ τόπῳ τῆς δεσποτείας σου. Σὺ γὰρ εἶ Θεὸς ἀνέκφραστος, ἀπερινόητος, ἀόρατος, ἀκατάληπτος, ἀεὶ ὤν, ὡσαύτως ὤν, σὺ καὶ ὁ μονογενής σου Υἱὸς καὶ τὸ Πνεῦμά σου τὸ Ἅγιον. Σὺ ἐκ τοῦ μὴ ὄντος εἰς τὸ εἶναι ἡμᾶς παρήγαγες, καὶ παραπεσόντας ἀνέστησας πάλιν, καὶ οὐκ ἀπέστης πάντα ποιῶν, ἕως ἡμᾶς εἰς τὸν οὐρανὸν ἀνήγαγες καὶ τὴν βασιλείαν σου ἐχαρίσω τὴν μέλλουσαν. Ὑπὲρ τούτων ἁπάντων εὐχαριστοῦμέν σοι καὶ τῷ μονογενεῖ σου Υἱῷ καὶ τῷ Πνεύματί σου τῷ Ἁγίῳ, ὑπὲρ πάντων ὧν ἴσμεν καὶ ὧν οὐκ ἴσμεν, τῶν φανερῶν καὶ ἀφανῶν εὐεργεσιῶν, τῶν εἰς ἡμᾶς γεγενημένων. Εὐχαριστοῦμέν σοι καὶ ὑπὲρ τῆς λειτουργίας ταύτης, ἣν ἐκ τῶν χειρῶν ἡμῶν δέξασθαι κατηξίωσας, καίτοι σοι παρεστήκασι χιλιάδες ἀρχαγγέλων καὶ μυριάδες ἀγγέλων, τὰ Χερουβεὶμ καὶ τὰ Σεραφείμ, ἑξαπτέρυγα, πολυόμματα, μετάρσια πτερωτά,

Ἱερεύς: Τὸν ἐπινίκιον ὕμνον ᾄδοντα, βοῶντα, κεκραγότα καὶ λέγοντα·

Λαός: **Ἅγιος, ἅγιος, ἅγιος, Κύριος Σαβαώθ· πλήρης ὁ οὐρανὸς καὶ ἡ γῆ τῆς δόξης σου. Ὡσαννὰ ἐν τοῖς ὑψίστοις· εὐλογημένος ὁ ἐρχόμενος ἐν ὀνόματι Κυρίου. Ὡσαννά, ὁ ἐν τοῖς ὑψίστοις.**

Ἱερεύς (χαμηλοφώνως): Μετὰ τούτων καὶ

People: **It is proper and right.**

Priest (in a low voice): It is proper and right to sing to You, bless You, praise You, thank You and worship You in all places of Your dominion; for You are God ineffable, beyond comprehension, invisible, beyond understanding, existing forever and always the same; You and Your only begotten Son and Your Holy Spirit. You brought us into being out of nothing, and when we fell, You raised us up again. You did not cease doing everything until You led us to heaven and granted us Your kingdom to come. For all these things we thank You and Your only begotten Son and Your Holy Spirit; for all things that we know and do not know, for blessings seen and unseen that have been bestowed upon us. We also thank You for this liturgy which You are pleased to accept from our hands, even though You are surrounded by thousands of Archangels and tens of thousands of Angels, by the Cherubim and Seraphim, six-winged, many-eyed, soaring with their wings,

Priest: Singing the victory hymn, proclaiming, crying out, and saying:

People: **Holy, holy, holy, Lord Sabaoth, heaven and earth are filled with Your glory. Hosanna in the highest. Blessed is He who comes in the name of the Lord. Hosanna to God in the highest.**

Priest (in a low voice): Together with these

ἡμεῖς τῶν μακαρίων δυνάμεων, Δέσποτα φιλάνθρωπε, βοῶμεν καὶ λέγομεν· Ἅγιος εἶ καὶ
πανάγιος, Σὺ καὶ ὁ μονογενής σου Υἱός, καὶ
τὸ Πνεῦμά σου τὸ Ἅγιον. Ἅγιος εἶ καὶ πανάγιος καὶ μεγαλοπρεπὴς ἡ δόξα σου· ὃς τὸν κόσμον σου οὕτως ἠγάπησας, ὥστε τὸν Υἱόν Σου
τὸν μονογενῆ δοῦναι, ἵνα πᾶς ὁ πιστεύων εἰς
αὐτὸν μὴ ἀπόληται, ἀλλ᾽ ἔχῃ ζωὴν αἰώνιον.
Ὃς ἐλθὼν καὶ πᾶσαν τὴν ὑπὲρ ἡμῶν οἰκονομίαν πληρώσας, τῇ νυκτὶ ᾗ παρεδίδετο, μᾶλ-
λον δὲ ἑαυτὸν παρεδίδου ὑπὲρ τῆς τοῦ κόσμου
ζωῆς, λαβὼν ἄρτον ἐν ταῖς ἁγίαις αὐτοῦ καὶ
ἀχράντοις καὶ ἀμωμήτοις χερσίν, εὐχαριστή-
σας καὶ εὐλογήσας, ἁγιάσας, κλάσας, ἔδωκε
τοῖς ἁγίοις αὐτοῦ μαθηταῖς καὶ ἀποστόλοις,
εἰπών·

Ἱερεύς: Λάβετε, φάγετε· τοῦτό μού ἐστι τὸ
Σῶμα, τὸ ὑπὲρ ὑμῶν κλώμενον εἰς ἄφεσιν
ἁμαρτιῶν.

Λαός: **Ἀμήν.**

Ἱερεύς (χαμηλοφώνως): Ὁμοίως καὶ τὸ ποτήριον μετὰ τὸ δειπνῆσαι λέγων·

Ἱερεύς: Πίετε ἐξ αὐτοῦ πάντες· τοῦτό ἐστι τὸ
Αἷμά μου, τὸ τῆς καινῆς Διαθήκης, τὸ ὑπὲρ
ὑμῶν καὶ πολλῶν ἐκχυνόμενον εἰς ἄφεσιν
ἁμαρτιῶν.

Λαός: **Ἀμήν.**

Ἱερεύς (χαμηλοφώνως): **Μεμνημένοι τοίνυν**

blessed powers, merciful Master, we also proclaim and say: You are holy and most holy, You and Your only begotten Son and Your Holy Spirit. You are holy and most holy, and sublime is Your glory. You so loved Your world that You gave Your only begotten Son so that whoever believes in Him should not perish, but have eternal life. He came and fulfilled the divine plan for us. On the night when He was delivered up, or rather when He gave Himself up for the life of the world, He took bread in His holy, pure, and blameless hands, gave thanks, blessed, sanctified, broke, and gave it to His holy disciples and apostles, saying:

Priest: Take, eat, this is my Body which is broken for you for the forgiveness of sins.

People: **Amen.**

Priest (in a low voice): Likewise, after supper, He took the cup, saying:

Priest: Drink of it all of you; this is my Blood of the new Covenant which is shed for you and for many for the forgiveness of sins.

People: **Amen.**

Priest (in a low voice): Remembering, therefore,

τῆς σωτηρίου ταύτης ἐντολῆς καὶ πάντων τῶν ὑπὲρ ἡμῶν γεγενημένων, τοῦ σταυροῦ, τοῦ τάφου, τῆς τριημέρου ἀναστάσεως, τῆς εἰς οὐρανοὺς ἀναβάσεως, τῆς ἐκ δεξιῶν καθέδρας, τῆς δευτέρας καὶ ἐνδόξου πάλιν παρουσίας.

Ἱερεύς: Τὰ σὰ ἐκ τῶν σῶν σοὶ προσφέρομεν κατὰ πάντα καὶ διὰ πάντα.

Λαός: **Σὲ ὑμνοῦμεν, σὲ εὐλογοῦμεν, σοὶ εὐχαριστοῦμεν, Κύριε, καὶ δεόμεθά σου, ὁ Θεὸς ἡμῶν.**

Ἱερεύς (χαμηλοφώνως): Ἔτι προσφέρομέν σοι τὴν λογικὴν ταύτην καὶ ἀναίμακτον λατρείαν καὶ παρακαλοῦμέν σε καὶ δεόμεθα καὶ ἱκετεύομεν. Κατάπεμψον τὸ Πνεῦμά σου τὸ Ἅγιον ἐφ᾽ ἡμᾶς καὶ ἐπὶ τὰ προκείμενα δῶρα ταῦτα.

Ἱερεύς: Καὶ ποίησον τὸν μὲν ἄρτον τοῦτον, τίμιον Σῶμα τοῦ Χριστοῦ σου.
Ἀμήν.

Ἱερεύς: Τὸ δὲ ἐν τῷ ποτηρίῳ τούτῳ, τίμιον Αἷμα τοῦ Χριστοῦ σου.
Ἀμήν.

Ἱερεύς: Μεταβαλὼν τῷ Πνεύματί σου τῷ Ἁγίῳ. Ἀμήν. Ἀμήν. Ἀμήν.

Ἱερεύς: Ὥστε γενέσθαι τοῖς μεταλαμβάνουσιν εἰς νῆψιν ψυχῆς, εἰς ἄφεσιν ἁμαρτιῶν, εἰς κοινωνίαν τοῦ Ἁγίου σου Πνεύματος, εἰς βασιλείας οὐρανῶν πλήρωμα, εἰς παρρησίαν τὴν πρὸς σέ, μὴ εἰς κρῖμα ἢ εἰς κατάκριμα. Ἔτι προσφέρομέν σοι τὴν λογικὴν ταύτην

this command of the Savior, and all that came to pass for our sake, the cross, the tomb, the resurrection on the third day, the ascension into heaven, the enthronement at the right hand of the Father, and the second, glorious coming.

Priest: We offer to You these gifts from Your own gifts in all and for all.

People: **We praise You, we bless You, we give thanks to You, and we pray to You, Lord our God.**

Priest (in a low voice): Once again we offer to You this spiritual worship without the shedding of blood, and we ask, pray, and entreat You: send down Your Holy Spirit upon us and upon these gifts here presented.

Priest: And make this bread the precious Body of Your Christ.
Amen.

Priest: And that which is in this cup the precious Blood of Your Christ.
Amen.

Priest: Changing them by Your Holy Spirit.
Amen. Amen. Amen.

Priest: So that they may be to those who partake of them for vigilance of soul, forgiveness of sins, communion of Your Holy Spirit, fulfillment of the kingdom of heaven, confidence before You, and not in judgment or condemnation. Again, we offer this spiritual worship for

λατρείαν, ὑπὲρ τῶν ἐν πίστει ἀναπαυσαμένων Προπατόρων, Πατέρων, Πατριαρχῶν, Προφητῶν, Ἀποστόλων, Κηρύκων, Εὐαγγελιστῶν, Μαρτύρων, Ὁμολογητῶν, Ἐγκρατευτῶν καὶ παντὸς πνεύματος δικαίου ἐν πίστει τετελειωμένου.

Ἱερεύς: Ἐξαιρέτως τῆς παναγίας, ἀχράντου, ὑπερευλογημένης, ἐνδόξου, δεσποίνης ἡμῶν Θεοτόκου καὶ ἀειπαρθένου Μαρίας.

Λαός: **Ἄξιόν ἐστιν ὡς ἀληθῶς, μακαρίζειν σε τὴν Θεοτόκον, τὴν ἀειμακάριστον καὶ παναμώμητον καὶ μητέρα τοῦ Θεοῦ ἡμῶν. Τὴν τιμιωτέραν τῶν Χερουβεὶμ καὶ ἐνδοξοτέραν ἀσυγκρίτως τῶν Σεραφείμ, τὴν ἀδιαφθόρως Θεὸν Λόγον τεκοῦσαν, τὴν ὄντως Θεοτόκον, σὲ μεγαλύνομεν.**

Ἱερεύς (χαμηλοφώνως): Τοῦ ἁγίου Ἰωάννου, προφήτου, προδρόμου καὶ βαπτιστοῦ· τῶν ἁγίων, ἐνδόξων καὶ πανευφήμων Ἀποστόλων· τοῦ ἁγίου (*Ὄνομα*) οὗ καὶ τὴν μνήμην ἐπιτελοῦμεν, καὶ πάντων σου τῶν Ἁγίων, ὧν ταῖς ἱκεσίαις ἐπίσκεψαι ἡμᾶς, ὁ Θεός. Καὶ μνήσθητι πάντων τῶν κεκοιμημένων ἐπ᾽ ἐλπίδι ἀναστάσεως, ζωῆς αἰωνίου (*καὶ μνημονεύει ἐνταῦθα ὀνομαστὶ ὧν βούλεται τεθνεώτων*) καὶ ἀνάπαυσον αὐτούς, ὁ Θεὸς ἡμῶν, ὅπου ἐπισκοπεῖ τὸ φῶς τοῦ προσώπου σου. Ἔτι παρακαλοῦμέν σε· μνήσθητι, Κύριε, πάσης ἐπισκοπῆς ὀρθοδόξων, τῶν ὀρθοτομούντων τὸν λόγον τῆς σῆς

those who repose in the faith, forefathers, fathers, patriarchs, prophets, apostles, preachers, evangelists, martyrs, confessors, ascetics, and for every righteous spirit made perfect in faith.

Priest: Especially for our most holy, pure, blessed, and glorious Lady, the Theotokos and ever virgin Mary.

People: **It is truly right to bless you, Theotokos, ever blessed, most pure, and mother of our God. More honorable than the Cherubim, and beyond compare more glorious than the Seraphim, without corruption you gave birth to God the Word. We magnify you, the true Theotokos.**

Priest (in a low voice): For Saint John the prophet, forerunner, and baptist; for the holy glorious and most honorable Apostles, for Saints(s) (*Name-s*) whose memory we commemorate today; and for all Your saints, through whose supplications, O God, bless us. Remember also all who have fallen asleep in the hope of resurrection unto eternal life. (*Here the priest commemorates the names of the deceased.*) And grant them rest, our God, where the light of Your countenance shines. Again, we ask You, Lord, remember all Orthodox bishops who rightly teach the word of Your truth, all pres-

ἀληθείας, παντὸς τοῦ πρεσβυτερίου, τῆς ἐν Χριστῷ διακονίας καὶ παντὸς ἱερατικοῦ τάγματος. Ἔτι προσφέρομέν σοι τὴν λογικὴν ταύτην λατρείαν ὑπὲρ τῆς οἰκουμένης· ὑπὲρ τῆς ἁγίας, καθολικῆς καὶ ἀποστολικῆς Ἐκκλησίας· ὑπὲρ τῶν ἐν ἀγνοίᾳ καὶ σεμνῇ πολιτείᾳ διαγόντων· καὶ ὑπὲρ τῶν ἀρχόντων ἡμῶν· δὸς αὐτοῖς Κύριε, εἰρηνικὴν τὴν ἐξουσίαν, ἵνα καὶ ἡμεῖς, ἐν τῇ γαλήνῃ αὐτῶν, ἤρεμον καὶ ἡσύχιον βίον διάγωμεν, ἐν πάσῃ εὐσεβείᾳ καὶ σεμνότητι.

Ἱερεύς: Ἐν πρώτοις, μνήσθητι, Κύριε τοῦ Ἀρχιεπισκόπου ἡμῶν (*Ὄνομα*) καὶ τοῦ Ἐπισκόπου ἡμῶν (*Ὄνομα*), οὕς χάρισαι ταῖς ἁγίαις σου Ἐκκλησίαις ἐν εἰρήνῃ σώους, ἐντίμους, ὑγιεῖς, μακροημερεύοντας καὶ ὀρθοτομοῦντας τὸν λόγον τῆς σῆς ἀληθείας.

*Ἱερεύς: Καὶ ὧν ἕκαστος κατὰ διάνοιαν ἔχει καὶ πάντων καὶ πασῶν.

Λαός: **Καὶ πάντων καὶ πασῶν.**

Ἱερεύς (χαμηλοφώνως): Μνήσθητι, Κύριε, τῆς πόλεως ταύτης, ἐν ᾗ παροικοῦμεν, καὶ πάσης πόλεως καὶ χώρας καὶ τῶν πίστει οἰκούντων ἐν αὐταῖς. Μνήσθητι, Κύριε, πλεόντων, ὁδοιπορούντων, νοσούντων, καμνόντων, αἰχμαλώτων καὶ τῆς σωτηρίας αὐτῶν. Μνήσθητι, Κύριε, τῶν καρποφορούντων καὶ καλλιεργούντων ἐν ταῖς ἁγίαις σου Ἐκκλησίαις καὶ μεμνη-

byters, all deacons in the service of Christ, and every one in holy orders. We also offer to You this spiritual worship for the whole world, for the holy, catholic, and apostolic Church, and for those living in purity and holiness. And for all those in public service; permit them, Lord, to serve and govern in peace that through the faithful conduct of their duties we may live peaceful and serene lives in all piety and holiness.

Priest: Above all, remember, Lord, our Archbishop (*Name*) and our Bishop (*Name*): Grant that they may serve Your holy churches in peace. Keep them safe, honorable, and healthy for many years, rightly teaching the word of Your truth.

**Priest:* Remember also, Lord, those whom each of us calls to mind and all your people.

People: **And all Your people.**

Priest (in a low voice): Remember, Lord, the city in which we live, every city and country, and the faithful who dwell in them. Remember, Lord, the travelers, the sick, the suffering, and the captives, granting them protection and salvation. Remember, Lord, those who do charitable work, who serve in Your holy churches, and who

μένων τῶν πενήτων καὶ ἐπὶ πάντας ἡμᾶς τὰ ἐλέη σου ἐξαπόστειλον.

Ἱερεύς: Καὶ δὸς ἡμῖν, ἐν ἑνὶ στόματι καὶ μιᾷ καρδίᾳ δοξάζειν καὶ ἀνυμνεῖν τὸ πάντιμον καὶ μεγαλοπρεπὲς ὄνομά σου, τοῦ Πατρὸς καὶ τοῦ Υἱοῦ καὶ τοῦ Ἁγίου Πνεύματος, νῦν καὶ ἀεὶ καὶ εἰς τοὺς αἰῶνας τῶν αἰώνων.

Λαός: **Ἀμήν.**

Ἱερεύς: Καὶ ἔσται τὰ ἐλέη τοῦ μεγάλου Θεοῦ καὶ Σωτῆρος ἡμῶν Ἰησοῦ Χριστοῦ, μετὰ πάντων ἡμῶν.

Λαός: **Καὶ μετὰ τοῦ Πνεύματός σου.**

* *Ἱερεύς:* Πάντων τῶν ἁγίων μνημονεύσαντες, ἔτι καὶ ἔτι ἐν εἰρήνῃ τοῦ Κυρίου δεηθῶμεν.

Λαὸς: **Κύριε, ἐλέησον.**

* *Ἱερεύς:* Ὑπὲρ τῶν προσκομισθέντων καὶ ἁγιασθέντων τιμίων δώρων, τοῦ Κυρίου δεηθῶμεν.

Λαὸς: **Κύριε, ἐλέησον.**

* *Ἱερεύς:* Ὅπως ὁ φιλάνθρωπος Θεὸς ἡμῶν, ὁ προσδεξάμενος αὐτὰ εἰς τὸ ἅγιον καὶ ὑπερουράνιον καὶ νοερὸν αὐτοῦ θυσιαστήριον, εἰς ὀσμὴν εὐωδίας πνευματικῆς, ἀντικατα-

care for the poor. And send Your mercy upon us all.

Priest: And grant that with one voice and one heart we may glorify and praise Your most honored and majestic name, of the Father and the Son and the Holy Spirit, now and forever and to the ages of ages.

People: **Amen.**

Priest: The mercy of our great God and Savior Jesus Christ be with all of you.

People: **And with your spirit.**

*Priest: Having remembered all the saints, let us again in peace pray to the Lord.

People: **Lord, have mercy.**

*Priest: For the precious Gifts offered and consecrated, let us pray to the Lord.

People: **Lord, have mercy.**

*Priest: That our loving God who has received them at His holy, heavenly, and spiritual altar as an offering of spiritual fragrance, may in return send upon us divine grace and the gift

πέμψῃ ἡμῖν τὴν θείαν χάριν καὶ τὴν δωρεὰν
τοῦ Ἁγίου Πνεύματος, δεηθῶμεν.

Λαός: **Κύριε, ἐλέησον.**

* *Ἱερεύς:* Τὴν ἑνότητα τῆς πίστεως καὶ τὴν
κοινωνίαν τοῦ Ἁγίου Πνεύματος αἰτησάμενοι, ἑαυτοὺς καὶ ἀλλήλους καὶ πᾶσαν
τὴν ζωὴν ἡμῶν Χριστῷ τῷ Θεῷ παραθώμεθα.

Λαός: **Σοί, Κύριε.**

Ἱερεὺς (χαμηλοφώνως): Σοὶ παρακατιθέμεθα
τὴν ζωὴν ἡμῶν ἅπασαν, καὶ τὴν ἐλπίδα,
Δέσποτα φιλάνθρωπε, καὶ παρακαλοῦμέν σε
καὶ δεόμεθα καὶ ἱκετεύομεν. Καταξίωσον ἡμᾶς
μεταλαβεῖν τῶν ἐπουρανίων σου καὶ φρικτῶν
Μυστηρίων ταύτης τῆς ἱερᾶς καὶ πνευματικῆς
Τραπέζης, μετὰ καθαροῦ συνειδότος, εἰς
ἄφεσιν ἁμαρτιῶν, εἰς συγχώρησιν πλημμελημάτων, εἰς Πνεύματος Ἁγίου κοινωνίαν, εἰς βασιλείας οὐρανῶν κληρονομίαν, εἰς παρρησίαν
τὴν πρὸς σέ, μὴ εἰς κρῖμα, ἢ εἰς κατάκριμα.

Ἱερεύς: Καὶ καταξίωσον ἡμᾶς, Δέσποτα,
μετὰ παρρησίας, ἀκατακρίτως, τολμᾶν ἐπι-
καλεῖσθαί σε τὸν ἐπουράνιον Θεόν, Πατέρα,
καὶ λέγειν:

ΚΥΡΙΑΚΗ ΠΡΟΣΕΥΧΗ

Λαός: **Πάτερ ἡμῶν, ὁ ἐν τοῖς οὐρανοῖς·
ἁγιασθήτω τὸ ὄνομά σου·**

of the Holy Spirit, let us pray.

People: **Lord, have mercy.**

*Priest: Having prayed for the unity of the faith and for the communion of the Holy Spirit, let us commit ourselves, and one another, and our whole life to Christ our God.

People: **To You, O Lord.**

> *Priest (in a low voice)*: We entrust to You, loving Master, our whole life and hope, and we ask, pray, and entreat: make us worthy to partake of your heavenly and awesome Mysteries from this holy and spiritual Table with a clear conscience; for the remission of sins, forgiveness of transgressions, communion of the Holy Spirit, inheritance of the kingdom of heaven, confidence before You, and not in judgment or condemnation.

Priest: And make us worthy, Master, with confidence and without fear of condemnation, to dare call You, the heavenly God, FATHER, and to say:

THE LORD'S PRAYER

People: **Our Father, who art in heaven, hallowed be Thy name.**

ἐλθέτω ἡ βασιλεία σου·
γενηθήτω τὸ θέλημά σου,
ὡς ἐν οὐρανῷ καὶ ἐπὶ τῆς γῆς.
Τὸν ἄρτον ἡμῶν τὸν ἐπιούσιον
δὸς ἡμῖν σήμερον·
καὶ ἄφες ἡμῖν τὰ ὀφειλήματα ἡμῶν,
ὡς καὶ ἡμεῖς ἀφίεμεν τοῖς ὀφειλέταις ἡμῶν·
καὶ μὴ εἰσενέγκῃς ἡμᾶς εἰς πειρασμόν,
ἀλλὰ ρῦσαι ἡμᾶς ἀπὸ τοῦ πονηροῦ.

Ἱερεύς: Ὅτι σοῦ ἐστιν ἡ βασιλεία καὶ ἡ
δύναμις καὶ ἡ δόξα, τοῦ Πατρὸς καὶ τοῦ Υἱοῦ
καὶ τοῦ Ἁγίου Πνεύματος, νῦν καὶ ἀεὶ καὶ
εἰς τοὺς αἰῶνας τῶν αἰώνων.

Λαός: **Ἀμήν.**

Ἱερεύς: Εἰρήνη πᾶσι.

Λαός: **Καὶ τῷ πνεύματί σου.**

*Ἱερεύς: Τὰς κεφαλὰς ἡμῶν τῷ Κυρίῳ κλί-
νωμεν.

Λαός: **Σοί, Κύριε.**

Ἱερεύς (χαμηλοφώνως): Εὐχαριστοῦμέν σοι,
Βασιλεῦ ἀόρατε, ὁ τῇ ἀμετρήτῳ σου δυνάμει
τὰ πάντα δημιουργήσας καὶ τῷ πλήθει τοῦ
ἐλέους σου ἐξ οὐκ ὄντων εἰς τὸ εἶναι παραγα-
γών. Αὐτὸς Δέσποτα, οὐρανόθεν ἔπιδε ἐπὶ
τοὺς ὑποκεκλικότας σοι τὰς ἑαυτῶν κεφαλάς.

Thy kingdom come;
Thy will be done,
on earth as it is in heaven.
Give us this day
our daily bread,
and forgive us our trespasses
as we forgive those who trespass against us,
and lead us not into temptation,
but deliver us from evil.

Priest: For Yours is the kingdom and the power and the glory of the Father and the Son and the Holy Spirit, now and forever and to the ages of ages.

People: **Amen.**

Priest: Peace be with all.

People: **And with your spirit.**

**Priest:* Let us bow our heads to the Lord.

People: **To You, O Lord.**

Priest (in a low voice): We give thanks to You, invisible King. By Your infinite power You created all things and by Your great mercy You brought everything from nothing into being. Master, look down from heaven upon those who have bowed their heads before You; they have

Οὐ γὰρ ἔκλιναν σαρκὶ καὶ αἵματι, ἀλλὰ σοί, τῷ φοβερῷ Θεῷ. Σὺ οὖν, Δέσποτα, τὰ προκείμενα πᾶσιν ἡμῖν εἰς ἀγαθὸν ἐξομάλισον, κατὰ τὴν ἑκάστου ἰδίαν χρείαν· τοῖς πλέουσι σύμπλευσον· τοῖς ὁδοιποροῦσι συνόδευσον· τοὺς νοσοῦντας ἴασαι, ὁ ἰατρὸς τῶν ψυχῶν καὶ τῶν σωμάτων ἡμῶν.

Ἱερεύς: Χάριτι καὶ οἰκτιρμοῖς καὶ φιλανθρωπίᾳ τοῦ μονογενοῦς σου Υἱοῦ, μεθ᾽ οὗ εὐλογητὸς εἶ, σὺν τῷ παναγίῳ καὶ ἀγαθῷ καὶ ζωοποιῷ σου Πνεύματι, νῦν καὶ ἀεὶ καὶ εἰς τοὺς αἰῶνας τῶν αἰώνων.

Λαός: **Ἀμήν.**

Η ΘΕΙΑ ΜΕΤΑΛΗΨΙΣ

Ἱερεύς (χαμηλοφώνως): Πρόσχες, Κύριε Ἰησοῦ Χριστέ, ὁ Θεὸς ἡμῶν, ἐξ ἁγίου κατοικητηρίου σου καὶ ἀπὸ θρόνου δόξης τῆς βασιλείας σου καὶ ἐλθὲ εἰς τὸ ἁγιάσαι ἡμᾶς, ὁ ἄνω τῷ Πατρὶ συγκαθήμενος καὶ ὧδε ἡμῖν ἀοράτως συνών. Καὶ καταξίωσον τῇ κραταιᾷ σου χειρὶ μεταδοῦναι ἡμῖν τοῦ ἀχράντου Σώματός σου καὶ τοῦ τιμίου Αἵματος, καὶ δι᾽ ἡμῶν παντὶ τῷ λαῷ.

* *Ἱερεύς:* Πρόσχωμεν.

Ἱερεύς: Τὰ ἅγια τοῖς ἁγίοις.

Λαός: **Εἷς ἅγιος, εἷς Κύριος, Ἰησοῦς Χριστός, εἰς δόξαν Θεοῦ Πατρός. Ἀμήν.**

bowed not before flesh and blood but before You the awesome God. Therefore, Master, guide the course of our life for our benefit according to the need of each of us. Sail with those who sail; travel with those who travel; and heal the sick, Physician of our souls and bodies.

Priest: By the grace, mercy, and love for us of Your only begotten Son, with whom You are blessed, together with Your all holy, good, and life giving Spirit, now and forever and to the ages of ages.

People: **Amen.**

HOLY COMMUNION

Priest (in a low voice): Lord Jesus Christ, our God, hear us from Your holy dwelling place and from the glorious throne of Your kingdom. You are enthroned on high with the Father and are also invisibly present among us. Come and sanctify us, and let Your pure Body and precious Blood be given to us by Your mighty hand and through us to all Your people.

*Priest: Let us be attentive.

Priest: The holy Gifts for the holy people of God.

People: **One is Holy, one is Lord, Jesus Christ, to the glory of God the Father. Amen.**

Ο ΚΟΙΝΩΝΙΚΟΣ ΥΜΝΟΣ

Λαός: **Αἰνεῖτε τὸν Κύριον ἐκ τῶν οὐρανῶν. Αἰνεῖτε αὐτὸν ἐν τοῖς ὑψίστοις. Ἀλληλούϊα** *(3). (Τὸ Κοινωνικὸν ἀλλάσσει κατὰ τὰς διαφόρους ἑορτάς.)*

* * *

Ἱερεύς (εὐθέως μελίζει τὸν ἅγιον Ἄρτον, λέγων χαμηλοφώνως): Μελίζεται καὶ διαμερίζεται ὁ Ἀμνὸς τοῦ Θεοῦ, ὁ μελιζόμενος καὶ μὴ διαιρούμενος· ὁ πάντοτε ἐσθιόμενος, καὶ μηδέποτε δαπανώμενος, ἀλλὰ τοὺς μετέχοντας ἁγιάζων.

(Λαβὼν ἐκ τοῦ ἄρτου μερίδα μίαν, βάλλει αὐτὴν εἰς τὸ ἅγιον Ποτήριον λέγων:) Πλήρωμα ποτηρίου πίστεως Πνεύματος Ἁγίου.

(Εὐλογεῖ τὸ Ζέον λέγων:) Εὐλογημένη ἡ ζέσις τῶν ἁγίων σου, πάντοτε· νῦν καὶ ἀεὶ καὶ εἰς τοὺς αἰῶνας τῶν αἰώνων. Ἀμήν.

(Ἐγχέει σταυροειδῶς τὸ Ζέον ἐν τῷ ποτηρίῳ λέγων·) Ζέσις Πνεύματος ἁγίου. Ἀμήν.

* * * * * * *

(Αἱ προσευχαὶ τῆς θείας Κοινωνίας λέγονται χαμηλοφώνως ἀπὸ ὅσους θὰ μεταλάβουν.)

Πιστεύω, Κύριε, καὶ ὁμολογῶ ὅτι σὺ εἶ ἀληθῶς ὁ Χριστός, ὁ Υἱὸς τοῦ Θεοῦ τοῦ ζῶντος, ὁ ἐλθὼν εἰς τὸν κόσμον ἁμαρτωλοὺς σῶσαι, ὧν πρῶτός εἰμι ἐγώ. Ἔτι πιστεύω ὅτι τοῦτο αὐτό ἐστι τὸ ἄχραντον Σῶμά σου καὶ τοῦτο αὐτὸ

THE COMMUNION HYMN

People: **Praise the Lord from the heavens; praise Him in the highest. Alleluia** (*3*).
(*The Communion Hymn changes according to the Feast Day.*)

* * *

Priest (After the fraction of the sacred Bread, the priest says in a low voice): The Lamb of God is broken and distributed; broken but not divided. He is forever eaten yet is never consumed, but He sanctifies those who partake of Him.

(*Then the priest places a portion of the sacred Bread in the Cup saying:*) The fullness of the Holy Spirit. Amen.

(*He then blesses the warm water saying:*) Blessed is the fervor of Your saints, now and forever and to the ages of ages. Amen.

(*Pouring the water into the Cup crosswise, he says:*) The warmth of the Holy Spirit. Amen.

* * * * * * *

(*The Communion Prayers are recited silently by those prepared to receive the holy Mysteries.*)

I believe and confess, Lord, that You are truly the Christ, the Son of the living God, who came into the world to save sinners, of whom I am the first. I also believe that this is truly Your pure

ἐστι τὸ τίμιον Αἷμά σου. Δέομαι οὖν σου· ἐλέη-
σόν με καὶ συγχώρησόν μοι τὰ παραπτώματά
μου, τὰ ἑκούσια καὶ τὰ ἀκούσια, τὰ ἐν λόγῳ,
τὰ ἐν ἔργῳ, τὰ ἐν γνώσει καὶ ἀγνοίᾳ· καὶ ἀξίωσόν με ἀκατακρίτως μετασχεῖν τῶν ἀχράντων
σου Μυστηρίων, εἰς ἄφεσιν ἁμαρτιῶν καὶ εἰς
ζωὴν αἰώνιον. Ἀμήν.

Ἐν ταῖς λαμπρότησι τῶν ἁγίων σου, πῶς εἰσε-
λεύσομαι ὁ ἀνάξιος; Ἐὰν γὰρ τολμήσω συνει-
σελθεῖν εἰς τὸν νυμφῶνα, ὁ χιτών με ἐλέγχει
ὅτι οὐκ ἔστι τοῦ γάμου, καὶ δέσμιος ἐκβαλοῦ-
μαι ὑπὸ τῶν Ἀγγέλων· καθάρισον, Κύριε, τὸν
ρύπον τῆς ψυχῆς μου, καὶ σῶσόν με, ὡς
φιλάνθρωπος.

Δέσποτα φιλάνθρωπε, Κύριε Ἰησοῦ Χριστέ, ὁ
Θεός μου, μὴ εἰς κρῖμά μοι γένοιτο τὰ ἅγια
ταῦτα διὰ τὸ ἀνάξιον εἶναί με, ἀλλ᾽ εἰς κάθαρ-
σιν καὶ ἁγιασμὸν ψυχῆς τε καὶ σώματος καὶ
εἰς ἀρραβῶνα μελλούσης ζωῆς καὶ βασιλείας.
Ἐμοὶ δὲ τὸ προσκολλᾶσθαι τῷ Θεῷ ἀγαθόν
ἐστι, τίθεσθαι ἐν Κυρίῳ τὴν ἐλπίδα τῆς σωτηρίας μου.

Τοῦ Δείπνου σου τοῦ μυστικοῦ, σήμερον, Υἱὲ
Θεοῦ, κοινωνόν με παράλαβε· οὐ μὴ γὰρ τοῖς
ἐχθροῖς σου τὸ μυστήριον εἴπω· οὐ φίλημά σοι
δώσω καθάπερ ὁ Ἰούδας· ἀλλ᾽ ὡς ὁ ληστὴς
ὁμολογῶ σοι· Μνήσθητί μου, Κύριε, ὅταν
ἔλθῃς ἐν τῇ βασιλείᾳ σου.

* * *

Body and that this is truly Your precious Blood. Therefore, I pray to You, have mercy upon me, and forgive my transgressions, voluntary and involuntary, in word and deed, known and unknown. And make me worthy without condemnation to partake of Your pure Mysteries for the forgiveness of sins and for life eternal. Amen.

How shall I, who am unworthy, enter into the splendor of Your saints? If I dare to enter into the bridal chamber, my clothing will accuse me, since it is not a wedding garment; and being bound up, I shall be cast out by the angels. In Your love, Lord, cleanse my soul and save me.

Loving Master, Lord Jesus Christ, my God, let not these holy Gifts be to my condemnation because of my unworthiness, but for the cleansing and sanctification of soul and body and the pledge of the future life and kingdom. It is good for me to cling to God and to place in Him the hope of my salvation.

Receive me today, Son of God, as a partaker of Your mystical Supper. I will not reveal Your mystery to Your adversaries. Nor will I give You a kiss as did Judas. But as the thief I confess to You: Lord, remember me in Your kingdom.

* * *

(Ὁ Ἱερεὺς ἑτοιμάζεται ἵνα μεταλάβῃ τῶν ἀχράντων Μυστηρίων.)

Ἱερεύς: Ἰδοὺ προσέρχομαι Χριστῷ τῷ ἀθανάτῳ βασιλεῖ καὶ Θεῷ ἡμῶν.

Μεταδίδοταί μοι (*Ὄνομα*) τῷ ἱερεῖ τὸ τίμιον καὶ πανάγιον Σῶμα τοῦ Κυρίου καὶ Θεοῦ, καὶ Σωτῆρος ἡμῶν Ἰησοῦ Χριστοῦ, εἰς ἄφεσίν μου ἁμαρτιῶν καὶ εἰς ζωὴν αἰώνιον.

(*Καὶ μεταλαμβάνει τοῦ ἁγίου Ἄρτου.*)

Ἔτι μεταδίδοταί μοι (*Ὄνομα*) τῶ ἱερεῖ τὸ τίμιον καὶ πανάγιον Αἷμα τοῦ Κυρίου καὶ Θεοῦ καὶ Σωτῆρος ἡμῶν Ἰησοῦ Χριστοῦ, εἰς ἄφεσίν μου ἁμαρτιῶν καὶ εἰς ζωὴν αἰώνιον.

(*Καὶ μεταλαμβάνει ἐκ τοῦ ἁγίου Ποτηρίου.*)

Τοῦτο ἥψατο τῶν χειλέων μου, καὶ ἀφελεῖ τὰς ἀνομίας μου καὶ τὰς ἁμαρτίας μου περικαθαριεῖ.

(*Εἶτα ὁ Ἱερεὺς τίθησι τὰς λοιπὰς μερίδας τοῦ τιμίου Ἄρτου εἰς τὸ ἅγιον Ποτήριον λέγων·*)

Ἀνάστασιν Χριστοῦ θεασάμενοι, προσκυνήσωμεν ἅγιον, Κύριον Ἰησοῦν, τὸν μόνον ἀναμάρτητον. Τὸν Σταυρόν σου, Χριστέ, προσκυνοῦμεν καὶ τὴν ἁγίαν σου ἀνάστασιν ὑμνοῦμεν καὶ δοξάζομεν· σὺ γὰρ εἶ Θεὸς ἡμῶν, ἐκτός σου ἄλλον οὐκ οἴδαμεν, τὸ ὄνομά σου ὀνομάζομεν. Δεῦτε πάντες οἱ πιστοὶ προσκυνήσωμεν τὴν τοῦ Χριστοῦ ἁγίαν ἀνάστασιν, ἰδοὺ γὰρ ἦλθε διὰ τοῦ Σταυροῦ, χαρὰ ἐν ὅλῳ τῷ κόσμῳ·

(The Priest prepares to receive holy Communion.)

Priest: **Behold, I approach Christ, our immortal King and God.**

The precious and most holy Body of our Lord, God, and Savior Jesus Christ is given to me *(Name)* **the priest, for the forgiveness of my sins and eternal life.**

(He then partakes of the sacred Bread.)

The precious and most holy Blood of our Lord, God, and Savior Jesus Christ is given to me *(Name)* **the priest, for the forgiveness of my sins and eternal life.**

(He then drinks from the Chalice.)

(Afterwards, he wipes the Chalice, kisses it, and says:) **This has touched my lips, taking away my transgressions and cleansing my sins.**

(The priest then transfers the remaining portions of the consecrated Bread into the Cup, saying:)

Having beheld the resurrection of Christ, let us worship the holy Lord Jesus, the only Sinless One. We venerate Your cross, O Christ, and we praise and glorify Your holy resurrection. You are our God. We know no other than You, and we call upon Your name. Come, all faithful, let us venerate the holy resurrection of Christ. For behold, through the cross joy has come to all the

διὰ παντὸς εὐλογοῦντες τὸν Κύριον, ὑμνοῦμεν
τὴν ἀνάστασιν αὐτοῦ· Σταυρὸν γὰρ ὑπομείνας
δι᾽ ἡμᾶς, θανάτῳ θάνατον ὤλεσεν.

* * *

*(Εἶτα ὁ ἱερεὺς λαμβάνει τὸ ἅγιον Ποτήριον καὶ
ἐξελθὼν εἰς τὴν θύραν καὶ ὑψῶν αὐτό, ἐκφωνεῖ·)*

**Ἱερεύς:* Μετὰ φόβου Θεοῦ, πίστεως καὶ ἀγά-
πης προσέλθετε.

*(Οἱ προητοιμασμένοι πιστοὶ προσέρχονται μετὰ
κατανύξεως καὶ μεταλαμβάνουν τῶν ἀχράντων
μυστηρίων ἐνῶ ὁ λαὸς συνεχίζει τὸ Κοινωνικόν.)*

(Μεταλαμβάνων τοὺς πιστοὺς ὁ ἱερεὺς λέγει·)

Μεταλαμβάνει ὁ δοῦλος τοῦ Θεοῦ *(ὄνομα)*
σῶμα καὶ αἷμα Χριστοῦ εἰς ἄφεσιν ἁμαρτιῶν
καὶ ζωὴν αἰώνιον.

*(Μετὰ τὴν μετάληψιν τῶν πιστῶν, ὁ ἱερεὺς εὐλο-
γεῖ τὸν λαὸν λέγων·)*

Ἱερεύς: Σῶσον, ὁ Θεός, τὸν λαόν σου καὶ εὐλόγησον τὴν κληρονομίαν σου.

Λαός: **Εἴδομεν τὸ φῶς τὸ ἀληθινόν, ἐλάβομεν
πνεῦμα ἐπουράνιον, εὕρομεν πίστιν ἀληθῆ,
ἀδιαίρετον Τριάδα προσκυνοῦντες· αὕτη γὰρ
ἡμᾶς ἔσωσεν.**

*Ἱερεύς (Ἐπιστρέφων εἰς τὴν Ἁγίαν Τράπεζαν
εἰσκομίζει ἐν τῷ Ἁγίῳ Ποτηρίῳ τὰς λοιπὰς*

world. Blessing the Lord always, let us praise His resurrection. For enduring the cross for us, He destroyed death by death.

* * *

(*He takes the holy Cup, comes to the Royal Doors, raises it and says:*)

Priest: Approach with the fear of God, faith, and love.

(*Those prepared come forth with reverence to receive Holy Communion while the people sing the communion hymn.*)

(*When administering Holy Communion, the priest says:*) The servant of God (*Name*) receives the Body and Blood of Christ for forgiveness of sins and eternal life.

(*When Communion has been given to all, the priest blesses the people with his hand, saying:*)

Priest: Save, O God, Your people and bless Your inheritance.

People: **We have seen the true light; we have received the heavenly Spirit; we have found the true faith, worshiping the undivided Trinity, for the Trinity has saved us.**

(*Having returned the Cup to the holy Table, the priest transfers the particles of the Theotokos*)

*μερίδας τῆς Θεοτόκου καὶ τῶν Ἁγίων. Εἰσκο-
μίζων δὲ τὰς μερίδας τῶν ζώντων καὶ τεθνεώτων, λέγει χαμηλοφώνως):* Ἀπόπλυνον, Κύριε,
τὰ ἁμαρτήματα τῶν ἐνθάδε μνημονευθέντων
δούλων σου τῷ Αἵματί σου τῷ ἁγίῳ·
πρεσβείαις τῆς Θεοτόκου καὶ πάντων σου τῶν
Ἁγίων.

Ἱερεύς (χαμηλοφώνως): Ὑψώθητι ἐπὶ τοὺς
οὐρανούς, ὁ Θεός, καὶ ἐπὶ πᾶσαν τὴν γῆν ἡ
δόξα σου (*3*).

(*Ὑψῶν τὸ ἅγιον Ποτήριον ὁ Ἱερεὺς λέγει χαμηλοφώνως ·*) Εὐλογητὸς ὁ Θεὸς ἡμῶν.

Ἱερεύς: Πάντοτε· νῦν καὶ ἀεὶ καὶ εἰς τοὺς
αἰῶνας τῶν αἰώνων.

Λαός: **Ἀμήν.**

Λαός: **Πληρωθήτω τὸ στόμα ἡμῶν αἰνέσεως,
Κύριε, ὅπως ἂν ὑμνήσωμεν τὴν δόξαν σου,
ὅτι ἠξίωσας ἡμᾶς τῶν ἁγίων σου μετασχεῖν
Μυστηρίων· τήρησον ἡμᾶς ἐν τῷ σῷ ἁγιασμῷ, ὅλην τὴν ἡμέραν μελετῶντας τὴν
δικαιοσύνην σου. Ἀλληλούϊα. Ἀλληλούϊα.
Ἀλληλούϊα.**

Η ΕΥΧΑΡΙΣΤΗΡΙΟΣ ΕΥΧΗ

*Ἱερεύς: Ὀρθοί· μεταλαβόντες τῶν θείων,
ἁγίων, ἀχράντων, ἀθανάτων, ἐπουρανίων καὶ
ζωοποιῶν, φρικτῶν τοῦ Χριστοῦ Μυστηρίων,
ἀξίως, εὐχαριστήσωμεν τῷ Κυρίῳ.

Λαός: **Κύριε, ἐλέησον.**

and the saints into the Chalice, and then those of the living and the dead saying:) Wash away, Lord, by Your holy Blood, the sins of all those commemorated through the intercessions of the Theotokos and all Your saints. Amen.

(*He covers the vessels and censes them saying:*) Be exalted, O God, above the heavens. Let Your glory be over all the earth (3).

(*He lifts the vessels and says in a low voice:*) Blessed is our God.

Priest (aloud): Always, now and forever and to the ages of ages.

People: **Amen.**

People: **Let our mouths be filled with Your praise, Lord, that we may sing of Your glory. You have made us worthy to partake of Your holy mysteries. Keep us in Your holiness, that all the day long we may meditate upon Your righteousness. Alleluia. Alleluia. Alleluia.**

PRAYER OF THANKSGIVING

*Priest: Let us be attentive. Having partaken of the divine, holy, pure, immortal, heavenly, life giving, and awesome Mysteries of Christ, let us worthily give thanks to the Lord.

People: **Lord, have mercy.**

*Ἱερεύς: Ἀντιλαβοῦ, σῶσον, ἐλέησον καὶ διαφύλαξον ἡμᾶς, ὁ Θεός, τῇ σῇ χάριτι.

Λαὸς: **Κύριε, ἐλέησον.**

*Ἱερεύς: Τὴν ἡμέραν πᾶσαν, τελείαν, ἁγίαν, εἰρηνικὴν καὶ ἀναμάρτητον αἰτησάμενοι, ἑαυτοὺς καὶ ἀλλήλους καὶ πᾶσαν τὴν ζωὴν ἡμῶν, Χριστῷ τῷ Θεῷ παραθώμεθα.

Λαός: **Σοί, Κύριε.**

Ἱερεύς (χαμηλοφώνως): Εὐχαριστοῦμέν σοι, Δέσποτα φιλάνθρωπε, εὐεργέτα τῶν ψυχῶν ἡμῶν, ὅτι καὶ τῇ παρούσῃ ἡμέρᾳ κατηξίωσας ἡμᾶς τῶν ἐπουρανίων σου καὶ ἀθανάτων Μυστηρίων. Ὀρθοτόμησον ἡμῶν τὴν ὁδόν, στήριξον πάντας ἡμᾶς ἐν τῷ φόβῳ σου· φρούρησον ἡμῶν τὴν ζωήν, ἀσφάλισαι ἡμῶν τὰ διαβήματα· εὐχαῖς καὶ ἱκεσίαις τῆς ἐνδόξου Θεοτόκου καὶ ἀειπαρθένου Μαρίας καὶ πάντων τῶν Ἁγίων σου.

Ἱερεύς: Ὅτι σὺ εἶ ὁ ἁγιασμὸς ἡμῶν, καὶ σοὶ τὴν δόξαν ἀναπέμπομεν, τῷ Πατρὶ καὶ τῷ Υἱῷ καὶ τῷ Ἁγίῳ Πνεύματι, νῦν καὶ ἀεὶ καὶ εἰς τοὺς αἰῶνας τῶν αἰώνων.

Λαός: **Ἀμήν.**

ΑΠΟΛΥΣΙΣ

Ἱερεύς: Ἐν εἰρήνῃ προέλθωμεν.

Priest: Help us, save us, have mercy upon us, and protect us, O God, by Your grace.

People: **Lord, have mercy.**

Priest: Having prayed for a perfect, holy, peaceful, and sinless, day, let us commit ourselves, and one another, and our whole life to Christ our God.

People: **To You, O Lord.**

Priest (in a low voice): We thank You, loving Master, benefactor of our souls, that on this day You have made us worthy once again of Your heavenly and immortal Mysteries. Direct our ways in the right path, establish us firmly in Your fear, guard our lives, and make our endeavors safe, through the prayers and supplications of the glorious Theotokos and ever virgin Mary and of all Your saints.

Priest: For You are our sanctification and to You we give glory, to the Father and the Son and the Holy Spirit, now and forever and to the ages of ages.

People: **Amen.**

THE DISMISSAL

Priest: Let us depart in peace.

Ἱερεύς: Τοῦ Κυρίου δεηθῶμεν.

Λαὸς: **Κύριε, ἐλέησον.**

Ἱερεύς: Ὁ εὐλογῶν τοὺς εὐλογοῦντάς σε, Κύριε, καὶ ἁγιάζων τοὺς ἐπὶ σοὶ πεποιθότας, σῶσον τὸν λαόν σου καὶ εὐλόγησον τὴν κληρονομίαν σου. Τὸ πλήρωμα τῆς Ἐκκλησίας σου φύλαξον, ἁγίασον τοὺς ἀγαπῶντας τὴν εὐπρέπειαν τοῦ οἴκου σου. Σὺ αὐτοὺς ἀντιδόξασον τῇ θεϊκῇ σου δυνάμει καὶ μὴ ἐγκαταλίπῃς ἡμᾶς τοὺς ἐλπίζοντας ἐπὶ σέ. Εἰρήνην τῷ κόσμῳ σου δώρησαι, ταῖς Ἐκκλησίαις σου, τοῖς ἱερεῦσι, τοῖς ἄρχουσι, τῷ στρατῷ καὶ παντὶ τῷ λαῷ σου. Ὅτι πᾶσα δόσις ἀγαθὴ καὶ πᾶν δώρημα τέλειον ἄνωθέν ἐστι καταβαῖνον ἐκ σοῦ τοῦ Πατρὸς τῶν φώτων· καὶ σοὶ τὴν δόξαν καὶ εὐχαριστίαν καὶ προσκύνησιν ἀναπέμπομεν, τῷ Πατρὶ καὶ τῷ Υἱῷ καὶ τῷ Ἁγίῳ Πνεύματι, νῦν καὶ ἀεὶ καὶ εἰς τοὺς αἰῶνας τῶν αἰώνων.

Λαός: **Ἀμήν.**

Εἴη τὸ ὄνομα Κυρίου εὐλογημένον ἀπὸ τοῦ νῦν καὶ ἕως τοῦ αἰῶνος (3).

Ἱερεὺς (προχωρῶν πρὸς τὴν Πρόθεσιν λέγει χαμηλοφώνως): Τὸ πλήρωμα τοῦ Νόμου καὶ τῶν προφητῶν αὐτὸς ὑπάρχων, Χριστὲ ὁ Θεὸς ἡμῶν, ὁ πληρώσας πᾶσαν τὴν πατρικὴν οἰκονομίαν, πλήρωσον χαρᾶς καὶ εὐφροσύνης τὰς

Priest: Let us pray to the Lord.

People: **Lord, have mercy.**

Priest: Lord, bless those who praise You and sanctify those who trust in You. Save Your people and bless Your inheritance. Protect the whole body of Your Church. Sanctify those who love the beauty of Your house. Glorify them in return by Your divine power, and do not forsake us who hope in You. Grant peace to Your world, to Your churches, to the clergy, to those in public service, to the armed forces, and to all Your people. For every good and perfect gift is from above, coming from You, the Father of lights. To You we give glory, thanksgiving, and worship, to the Father and the Son and the Holy Spirit, now and forever and to the ages of ages.

People: **Amen.**

Blessed is the name of the Lord, both now and to the ages (*3*).

(*The priest proceeds to the Prothesis and prays in a low voice:*) Christ our God, You are the fulfillment of the Law and the Prophets. You have fulfilled all the dispensation of the Father. Fill our hearts with joy and gladness always, now

καρδίας ἡμῶν πάντοτε, νῦν καὶ ἀεὶ καὶ εἰς τοὺς αἰῶνας τῶν αἰώνων. Ἀμήν.

Ἱερεύς: Τοῦ Κυρίου δεηθῶμεν.

Λαὸς: **Κύριε, ἐλέησον** (3). **Πάτερ ἅγιε, εὐλόγησον.**

Ἱερεύς: Εὐλογία Κυρίου καὶ ἔλεος ἔλθοι ἐφ᾽ ὑμᾶς τῇ αὐτοῦ θείᾳ χάριτι καὶ φιλανθρωπίᾳ πάντοτε, νῦν καὶ ἀεὶ καὶ εἰς τοὺς αἰῶνας τῶν αἰώνων.

Λαός: **Ἀμήν.**

Ἱερεύς: Δόξα σοι ὁ Θεός, ἡ ἐλπὶς ἡμῶν, δόξα σοι.

Ἱερεύς: (Ὁ ἀναστὰς ἐκ νεκρῶν) [1] Χριστὸς ὁ ἀληθινὸς Θεὸς ἡμῶν, ταῖς πρεσβείαις τῆς παναχράντου καὶ παναμώμου ἁγίας αὐτοῦ μητρός· δυνάμει τοῦ τιμίου καὶ ζωοποιοῦ Σταυροῦ· προστασίαις τῶν τιμίων ἐπουρανίων Δυνάμεων ἀσωμάτων· ἱκεσίαις τοῦ τιμίου, ἐνδόξου, προφήτου, προδρόμου καὶ βαπτιστοῦ Ἰωάννου· τῶν ἁγίων, ἐνδόξων καὶ πανευφήμων Ἀποστόλων· τῶν ἁγίων, ἐνδόξων καὶ καλλινίκων Μαρτύρων· τῶν ὁσίων

---

[1] (*Παραλείπεται κατὰ τὰς καθημερινὰς Λειτουργίας*)

and forever and to the ages of ages. Amen.

Priest: Let us pray to the Lord.

People: **Lord, have mercy** (*3*). **Father, give the blessing.**

Priest: May the blessing of the Lord and His mercy come upon you through His divine grace and love always, now and forever and to the ages of ages.

People: **Amen.**

Priest: Glory to You, O God, our hope, glory to you.

Priest: May Christ our true God (who rose from the dead),[1] as a good, loving, and merciful God, have mercy upon us and save us, through the intercessions of His most pure and holy Mother; the power of the precious and life-giving Cross; the protection of the honorable, bodiless powers of heaven, the supplications of the honorable, glorious prophet and forerunner John the Baptist; the holy, glorious and praiseworthy apostles; the holy, glorious and

---

[1](*Omitted during weekday Liturgies.*)

καὶ θεοφόρων Πατέρων ἡμῶν (τοῦ Ναοῦ)·
τῶν ἁγίων καὶ δικαίων θεοπατόρων Ἰωακεὶμ
καὶ Ἄννης, τοῦ Ἁγίου (τῆς ἡμέρας) οὗ καὶ
τὴν μνήμην ἐπιτελοῦμεν, καὶ πάντων τῶν
ἁγίων, ἐλεῆσαι καὶ σῶσαι ἡμᾶς ὡς ἀγαθὸς
καὶ φιλάνθρωπος καὶ ἐλεήμων Θεός.

Λαός: **Ἀμήν.**

Λαός: **Τὸν εὐλογοῦντα καὶ ἁγιάζοντα ἡμᾶς,
Κύριε φύλαττε εἰς πολλὰ ἔτη.**

Ἱερεύς: Δι᾽ εὐχῶν τῶν ἁγίων Πατέρων ἡμῶν,
Κύριε Ἰησοῦ Χριστέ, ὁ Θεὸς ἡμῶν, ἐλέησον
καὶ σῶσον ἡμᾶς.[1]

Λαός: **Ἀμήν.**

Ἱερεὺς (εὐλογῶν τὸν λαόν): Ἡ ἁγία Τριὰς δι-
αφυλάξοι πάντας ὑμᾶς.

*(Προσφερομένου δὲ τοῦ ἀντιδώρου ὁ Ἱερεὺς
λέγει·)*

Εὐλογία Κυρίου καὶ ἔλεος ἔλθοι ἐπὶ σέ.

---

[1]*(Κατὰ τὴν Πασχάλιον περίοδον λέγεται τὸ «Χριστὸς Ἀνέστη . . . »)*

triumphant martyrs; our holy and God-bearing Fathers (*name of the church*); the holy and righteous ancestors Joachim and Anna; Saint (*of the day*) whose memory we commemorate today, and all the saints.

People: **Amen.**

People: **Lord, grant long life to him who blesses and sanctifies us.**

Priest: Through the prayers of our holy fathers, Lord Jesus Christ, our God, have mercy on us and save us.[1]

People: **Amen.**

Priest (blessing the people): May the holy Trinity protect all of you.

(*Distributing the antidoron, the priest says:*)

May the blessing and the mercy of the Lord be with you.

---

[1](*During the Paschal period, the priest says instead "Christ is risen . . ."*)

ΕΥΧΑΡΙΣΤΙΑ ΜΕΤΑ ΤΗΝ ΘΕΙΑΝ ΜΕΤΑΛΗΨΙΝ

THANKSGIVING FOLLOWING HOLY COMMUNION

ΕΥΧΑΡΙΣΤΙΑ ΜΕΤΑ ΤΗΝ ΘΕΙΑΝ ΜΕΤΑΛΗΨΙΝ

Δόξα σοι, ὁ Θεὸς ἡμῶν, δόξα σοι.
Δόξα σοι, ὁ Θεὸς ἡμῶν, δόξα σοι.
Δόξα σοι, ὁ Θεὸς ἡμῶν, δόξα σοι.

ΑΝΩΝΥΜΟΥ

Τὸ σῶμα σου τὸ ἅγιον, Κύριε Ἰησοῦ Χριστὲ ὁ Θεὸς ἡμῶν, γένοιτό μοι εἰς ζωὴν αἰώνιον καὶ τὸ Αἷμά σου τὸ τίμιον, εἰς ἄφεσιν ἁμαρτιῶν. Γένοιτο δέ μοι ἡ εὐχαριστία αὕτη εἰς χαράν, ὑγείαν καὶ εὐφροσύνην· καὶ ἐν τῇ φοβερᾷ ἐλεύσει σου ἀξίωσόν με τὸν ἁμαρτωλὸν στῆναι ἐκ δεξιῶν τῆς σῆς δόξης· πρεσβείαις τῆς παναχράντου σου Μητρὸς καὶ πάντων σου τῶν Ἁγίων. Ἀμήν.

ΜΕΓΑΛΟΥ ΒΑΣΙΛΕΙΟΥ

Δέσποτα Χριστὲ ὁ Θεός, Βασιλεῦ τῶν αἰώνων καὶ δημιουργὲ τῶν ἁπάντων, εὐχαριστῶ σοι ἐπὶ πᾶσιν οἷς παρέσχου μοι ἀγαθοῖς καὶ ἐπὶ τῇ μεταλήψει τῶν ἀχράντων καὶ ζωοποιῶν σου μυστηρίων. Δέομαι οὖν σου, ἀγαθὲ καὶ φιλάνθρωπε, φύλαξόν με ὑπὸ τὴν σκέπην σου καὶ ἐν τῇ τῶν πτερύγων σου σκιᾷ· καὶ δώρησαί μοι ἐν καθαρῷ συνειδότι, μέχρις ἐσχάτης μου ἀναπνοῆς, ἐπαξίως μετέχειν

THANKSGIVING FOLLOWING HOLY COMMUNION

Glory to you, our Lord, glory to you.
Glory to you, our Lord, glory to you.
Glory to you, our Lord, glory to you.

ANONYMOUS

Lord Jesus Christ, my God, let Your sacred Body be unto me for eternal life and Your precious Blood for forgiveness of sins. Let this Eucharist be unto me for joy, health and gladness. And in Your awesome Second Coming make me, a sinner, worthy to stand at the right hand of Your glory; through the intercessions of Your pure Mother and of all Your Saints. Amen.

SAINT BASIL

I thank You, Christ and Master our God, King of the ages and Creator of all things, for all the good gifts You have given me, and especially for the participation in Your pure and life-giving mysteries. I pray You, therefore, good and loving Lord, keep me under Your protection and under the shadow of Your wings. Grant that to my last breath I may with a pure conscience partake worthily of Your

τῶν ἁγιασμάτων σου, εἰς ἄφεσιν ἁμαρτιῶν καὶ εἰς ζωὴν αἰώνιον. Σὺ γὰρ εἶ ὁ ἄρτος τῆς ζωῆς, ἡ πηγὴ τοῦ ἁγιασμοῦ, ὁ δοτὴρ τῶν ἀγαθῶν· καὶ σοὶ τὴν δόξαν ἀναπέπομπεν, σὺν τῷ Πατρὶ καὶ τῷ Ἁγίῳ Πνεύματι, νῦν καὶ ἀεὶ καὶ εἰς τοὺς αἰῶνας τῶν αἰώνων. Ἀμήν.

ΑΝΩΝΥΜΟΥ

Εὐχαριστῶ σοι, Κύριε, ὁ Θεός μου, ὅτι οὐκ ἀπώσω με τὸν ἁμαρτωλόν, ἀλλὰ κοινωνόν με γενέσθαι τῶν ἁγιασμάτων σου κατηξίωσας. Εὐχαριστῶ σοι, ὅτι με τὸν ἀνάξιον μεταλαβεῖν τῶν ἀχράντων σου καὶ ἐπουρανίων δωρεῶν κατηξίωσας. Ἀλλὰ Δέσποτα φιλάνθρωπε, ὁ ὑπὲρ ἡμῶν ἀποθανών τε καὶ ἀναστὰς καὶ χαρισάμενος ἡμῖν τὰ φρικτὰ ταῦτα καὶ ζωοποιὰ σου Μυστήρια ἐπ᾽ εὐεργεσίᾳ καὶ ἁγιασμῷ τῶν ψυχῶν καὶ τῶν σωμάτων ἡμῶν, δὸς γενέσθαι ταῦτα κἀμοὶ εἰς ἴασιν ψυχῆς τε καὶ σώματος, εἰς ἀποτροπὴν παντὸς ἐναντίου, εἰς φωτισμὸν τῶν ὀφθαλμῶν τῆς καρδίας μου, εἰς εἰρήνη τῶν ψυχικῶν μου δυνάμεων, εἰς πίστιν ἀκαταίσχυντον, εἰς ἀγάπην ἀνυπόκριτον, εἰς πλησμονὴν σοφίας, εἰς περιποίησιν τῶν ἐντολῶν σου, εἰς προσθήκην τῆς θείας σου χάριτος καὶ τῆς βασιλείας οἰκείωσιν· ἵνα ἐν τῷ ἁγιασμῷ σου δι᾽ αὐτῶν φυλαττόμενος, τῆς σῆς χάριτος μνημονεύω διὰ παντὸς καὶ μηκέτι ἐμαυτῷ ζῶ, ἀλλὰ σοὶ τῷ ἡμετέρῳ Δεσπότῃ καὶ εὐεργέτῃ. Καὶ οὕτω, τοῦ τῇδε

gifts for the forgiveness of sins and for eternal
life. For You are the bread of life, the source
of holiness, the giver of all good things, and
to You we give glory, with the Father and the
Holy Spirit, now and forever and to the ages
of ages. Amen.

ANONYMOUS

I thank You, Lord my God, that You have
not rejected me, a sinner, but have made
me worthy to partake of Your holy mysteries.
I thank You that You have permitted me, although I am unworthy, to receive Your pure
and heavenly gifts. O loving Master, who died
and rose for our sake, and granted to us these
awesome and life-giving mysteries for the well-
being and sanctification of our souls and
bodies, let these gifts be for healing of my
own soul and body, the averting of every evil,
the illumination of the eyes of my heart, the
peace of my spiritual powers, a faith un-
ashamed, a love unfeigned, the fulfilling of
wisdom, the observing of Your commandments, the receiving of Your divine grace,
and the inheritance of Your kingdom. Pre-
served by them in Your holiness, may I always be mindful of Your grace and no longer
live for myself, but for You, our Master and
Benefactor. May I pass from this life in the
hope of eternal life, and attain to the everlasting rest, where the voices of Your Saints

βίου ἀπάρας ἐπ᾽ ἐλπίδι ζωῆς αἰωνίου, εἰς τὴν ἀΐδιον καταντήσω ἀνάπαυσιν, ἔνθα ὁ τῶν ἑορταζόντων ἦχος ὁ ἀκατάπαυστος καὶ ἡ ἀπέραντος ἡδονή τῶν καθορώντων τοῦ σοῦ προσώπου τὸ κάλλος τὸ ἄρρητον. Σὺ γὰρ εἶ τὸ ὄντως ἐφετόν, καὶ ἡ ἀνέκφραστος εὐφροσύνη τῶν ἀγαπώντων σε, Χριστὲ ὁ Θεὸς ἡμῶν, καὶ σὲ ὑμνεῖ πᾶσα ἡ κτῖσις εἰς τοὺς αἰῶνας. Ἀμήν.

ΙΩΑΝΝΟΥ ΤΟΥ ΧΡΥΣΟΣΤΟΜΟΥ

Εὐχαριστοῦμέν σοι, Δέσποτα φιλάνθρωπε, εὐεργέτα τῶν ψυχῶν ἡμῶν, ὅτι καὶ τῇ παρούσῃ ἡμέρᾳ κατηξίωσας ἡμᾶς τῶν ἐπουρανίων σου καὶ ἀθανάτων Μυστηρίων. Ὀρθοτόμησον ἡμῶν τὴν ὁδόν, στήριξον πάντας ἡμᾶς ἐν τῷ φόβῳ σου· φρούρησον ἡμῶν τὴν ζωήν, ἀσφάλισαι ἡμῶν τὰ διαβήματα· εὐχαῖς καὶ ἱκεσίαις τῆς ἐνδόξου Θεοτόκου καὶ ἀειπαρθένου Μαρίας καὶ πάντων τῶν Ἁγίων σου. Ἀμήν.

who feast are unceasing, and their joy, be-
holding the ineffable beauty of Your countenance, is unending. For You, Christ our God,
are the true joy and gladness of those who love
You, and all creation praises You forever.
Amen.

SAINT JOHN CHRYSOSTOMOS

I thank You, loving Master, benefactor of my
soul, that on this day You have made me worthy once again of Your heavenly and immortal mysteries. Direct my ways on the right path,
establish me firmly in Your fear, guard my life,
and make my endeavors safe, through the
prayers and supplications of the glorious Theotokos and ever virgin Mary and of all Your
Saints. Amen.

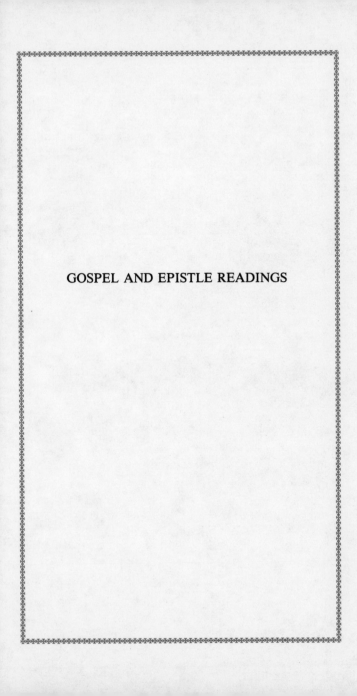

GOSPEL AND EPISTLE READINGS

SUNDAY OF EASTER

Verse: Give thanks to the Lord, for he is good;
for his mercy endures forever.

The reading is from the Acts of the Apostles.
Chapter 1.1-8.

In the first book, O Theophilos, I have dealt with all that Jesus began to do and teach, until the day when he was taken up, after he had given commandment through the Holy Spirit to the apostles whom he had chosen. To them he presented himself alive after his passion by many proofs, appearing to them during forty days, and speaking of the kingdom of God. And while staying with them he charged them not to depart from Jerusalem, but to wait for the promise of the Father, which, he said, "you heard from me, for John baptized with water, but before many days you shall be baptized with the Holy Spirit."

So when they had come together, they asked him, "Lord, will you at this time restore the kingdom to Israel?" He said to them, "It is not for you to know times or seasons which the Father has fixed by his own authority. But you shall receive power when the Holy Spirit has come upon you; and you shall be my witnesses in Jerusalem and in all Judea and Samaria and to the end of the earth."

THE GOSPEL READING
John 1.1-17.

In the beginning was the Word, and the Word was with God, and the Word was God. He was in the

45

beginning with God; all things were made through him, and without him was not anything made that was made. In him was life, and the life was the light of men. The light shines in the darkness, and the darkness has not overcome it.

There was a man sent from God, whose name was John. He came for testimony, to bear witness to the light, that all might believe through him. He was not the light, but came to bear witness to the light.

The true light that enlightens every man was coming into the world. He was in the world, and the world was made through him, yet the world knew him not. He came to his own home, and his own people received him not. But to all who received him, who believed in his name, he gave power to become children of God; who were born, not of blood nor of the will of the flesh nor of the will of man, but of God.

And the Word became flesh and dwelt among us, full of grace and truth; we have beheld his glory, glory as of the only Son from the Father. (John bore witness to him, and cried, "This was he of whom I said, 'He who comes after me ranks before me, for he was before me.'") And from his fulness have we all received, grace upon grace. For the law was given through Moses; grace and truth came through Jesus Christ.

SUNDAY OF SAINT THOMAS

Verse: Great is our Lord, and great is his power.
Praise the Lord, for the Lord is good.
The reading is from the Acts of the Apostles.

In those days many signs and wonders were done among the people by the hands of the apostles. And they were all together in Solomon's Portico. None of the rest dared join them, but the people held them in high honor. And more than ever believers were added to the Lord, multitudes both of men and women, so that they even carried out the sick into the streets, and laid them on beds and pallets, that as Peter came by at least his shadow might fall on some of them. The people also gathered from the towns around Jerusalem, bringing the sick and those afflicted with unclean spirits, and they were all healed.

But the high priest rose up and all who were with him, that is, the party of the Sadducees, and filled with jealousy they arrested the apostles and put them in the common prison. But at night an angel of the Lord opened the prison doors and brought them out and said, "Go and stand in the temple and speak to the people all the words of this Life."

THE GOSPEL READING
John 20.19-31.

On the evening of that day, the first day of the week, the doors being shut where the disciples were, for fear of the Jews, Jesus came and stood among them and said to them, "Peace be with you." When he had said this, he showed them his hands and his side. Then the disciples were glad when they saw the Lord. Jesus said to them again, "Peace be with you. As the Father has sent me, even so I send you." And when he had said this, he breathed on them, and said to them, "Receive the Holy Spirit. If you forgive the sins of any, they are forgiven; if you retain the sins of any, they are retained."

Now Thomas, one of the twelve, called the Twin, was not with them when Jesus came. So the other disciples told him, "We have seen the Lord." But he said to them, "Unless I see in his hands the print of the nails, and place my hand in his side, I will not believe."

Eight days later, his disciples were again in the house, and Thomas was with them. The doors were shut, but Jesus came and stood among them, and said, "Peace be with you." Then he said to Thomas, "Put your finger here, and see my hands; do not be faithless, but believing." Thomas answered him, "My Lord and my God!" Jesus said to him, "Have you believed because you have seen me? Blessed are those who have not seen and yet believe."

Now Jesus did many other signs in the presence of the disciples, which are not written in this book; but these are written that you may believe that Jesus is the Christ, the Son of God, and that believing you may have life in his name.

SUNDAY OF THE MYRRH-BEARERS

Verse: The Lord is my strength and my song.
The Lord has chastened me sorely.
The reading is from the Acts of the Apostles.
Chapter 6.1-7.
In those days, when the disciples were increasing in

number, the Hellenists murmured against the Hebrews because their widows were neglected in the daily distribution. And the twelve summoned the body of the disciples and said, "It is not right that we should give up preaching the word of God to serve tables. Therefore, brethren, pick out from among you seven men of good repute, full of the Spirit and of wisdom, whom we may appoint to this duty. But we will devote ourselves to prayer and to the ministry of the word." And what they said pleased the whole multitude, and they chose Stephen, a man full of faith and of the Holy Spirit, and Philip, and Prochoros, and Nicanor, and Timon, and Parmenas, and Nicolaos, a proselyte of Antioch. These they set before the apostles, and they prayed and laid their hands upon them.

THE GOSPEL READING
Mark 15.43-47; 16.1-8.

At that time, Joseph of Armathea, a respected member of the council, who was also himself looking for the kingdom of God, took courage and went to Pilate, and asked for the body of Jesus. And Pilate wondered if he were already dead; and summoning the centurion, he asked him whether he was already dead. And when he learned from the centurion that he was dead, he granted the body to Joseph. And he bought a linen shroud, and taking him down, wrapped him in the linen shroud, and laid him in a tomb which had been hewn out of the rock; and he rolled a stone against the door of the tomb. Mary Magdalene and Mary the mother of Joses saw where he was laid.

49

And when the sabbath was past, Mary Magdalene, and Mary the mother of James, and Salome, bought spices, so that they might go and anoint him. And very early on the first day of the week they went to the tomb when the sun had risen. And they were saying to one another, "Who will roll away the stone for us from the door of the tomb?" And looking up, they say that the stone was rolled back; for it was very large. And entering the tomb, they saw a young man sitting on the right side, dressed in a white robe; and they were amazed. And he said to them, "Do not be amazed; you seek Jesus of Nazareth, who was crucified. He has risen, he is not here; see the place where they laid him. But go, tell his disciples and Peter that he is going before you to Galilee; there you will see him, as he told you." And they went out and fled from the tomb; for trembling and astonishment had come upon them; and they said nothing to anyone, for they were afraid.

SUNDAY OF THE PARALYTIC

Verse: Sing praises to our God, sing praises.
Clap your hands, all you nations.
The reading is from the Acts of the Apostles.
Chapter 9.32-42.

In those days, as Peter went here and there among them all, he came down also to the saints that lived at Lydda. There he found a man named Aeneas, who had been bedridden for eight years and was paralyzed. And Peter said to him, "Aeneas, Jesus Christ heals you; rise and make your bed." And immediately he rose. And all the residents of Lydda and Sharon saw him, and they turned to the Lord.

Now there was at Joppa a disciple named Tabitha, which means Dorcas. She was full of good works and acts of charity. In those days she fell sick and died; and when they had washed her, they laid her in an upper room. Since Lydda was near Joppa, the disciples, hearing that Peter was there, sent two men to him entreating him, "Please come to us without delay." So Peter rose and went with them. And when he had come, they took him to the upper room. All the widows stood beside him weeping, and showing tunics and other garments which Dorcas made while she was with them. But Peter put them all outside and knelt down and prayed; then turning to the body he said, "Tabitha, rise." And she opened her eyes, and when she saw Peter she sat up. And he gave her his hand and lifted her up. Then calling the saints and widows he presented her alive. And it became known throughout all Joppa, and many believed in the Lord.

THE GOSPEL READING
John 5.1-15.

At that time, Jesus went up to Jerusalem. Now there is in Jerusalem by the Sheep Gate a pool, in Hebrew called Bethesda which has five porticoes. In these lay a multitude of invalids, blind, lame, paralyzed, waiting for the moving of the water; for an angel of the Lord went down at certain seasons into the pool, and troubled the water; whoever stepped in first after the troubling of the water was healed of whatever disease

51

he had. One man was there, who had been ill for thirty-eight years. When Jesus saw him and knew that he had been lying there for along time, he said to him, "Do you want to be healed?" The sick man answered him, "Sir, I have no man to put me into the pool when the water is troubled, and while I am going another steps down before me." Jesus said to him, "Rise, take up your pallet, and walk." And at once the man took up his pallet and walked.

Now that day was the sabbath. So the Jews said to the man who was cured, "It is the sabbath, it is not lawful for you to carry your pallet." But he answered them. "The man who healed me said to me, 'Take up your pallet, and walk.' " They asked him, "Who is the man who said to you, 'Take up your pallet and walk?' " Now the man who had been healed did not know who it was, for Jesus had withdrawn, as there was crowd in the place. Afterward, Jesus found him in the temple, and said to him, "See, you are well! Sin no more, that nothing worse befall you." The man went away and told the Jews that it was Jesus who had healed him.

SUNDAY OF THE SAMARITAN WOMAN

Verse: O Lord, how magnificent are your works.
You have made all things in wisdom.
Bless the Lord, O my soul.
The reading is from the Acts of the Apostles.
Chapter 11.19-30.
In those days, those apostles who were scattered

because of the persecution that arose over Stephen traveled as far as Phoenicia and Cyprus and Antioch, speaking the word to none except Jews. But there were some of them, men of Cyprus and Cyrene, who on coming to Antioch spoke to the Greeks also, preaching the Lord Jesus. And the hand of the Lord was with them, and a great number that believed turned to the Lord. News of this came to the ears of the church in Jerusalem, and they sent Barnabas to Antioch. When he came and saw the grace of God, he was glad; and he exhorted them to remain faithful to the Lord with steadfast purpose; for he was a good man, full of the Holy Spirit and of faith. And a large company was added to the Lord. So Barnabas went to Tarsus to look for Saul; and when he had found him, he brought him to Antioch. For a whole year they met with the church, and taught a large company of people; and in Antioch the disciples were for the first time called Christians.

Now in these days prophets came down from Jerusalem to Antioch. And one of them name Agabos stood up and foretold by the Spirit that there would be a great famine over all the world; and this took place in the days of Claudius. And the disciples determined, every one according to his ability, to send relief to the brethren who lived in Judea; and they did so, sending it to the elders by the hand of Barnabas and Saul.

THE GOSPEL READING
John 4.5-42.
At that time Jesus came to a city of Samaria, called

Sychar, near the field that Jacob gave to his son Joseph. Jacob's well was there, and so Jesus, wearied as he was with his journey, sat down beside the well. It was about the sixth hour.

There came a woman of Samaria to draw water. Jesus said to her, "Give me a drink." For his disciples had gone away into the city to buy food. The Samaritan woman said to him, "How is it that you, a Jew, ask a drink of me, a woman of Samaria?" For Jews have no dealings with Samaritans. Jesus answered her, "If you knew the gift of God, and who it is that is saying to you, 'Give me a drink,' you would have asked him and he would have given you living water." The woman said to him, "Sir, you have nothing to draw with, and the well is deep; where do you get that living water? Are you greater than our father Jacob, who gave us the well, and drank from it himself, and his sons, and his cattle?" Jesus said to her, "Everyone who drinks of this water will thirst again, but whoever drinks of the water that I shall give him will never thirst; the water that I shall give him will become in him a spring of water welling up to eternal life." The woman said to him, "Sir, give me this water, that I may not thirst, nor come here to draw."

Jesus said to her, "Go, call your husband, and come here." The woman answered him, "I have no husband." Jesus said to her, "You are right in saying, 'I have no husband'; for you have had five husbands, and he whom you now have is not your husband; this you said truly." The woman said to him, "Sir, I perceive that you are a prophet. Our fathers worshiped on this mountain; and you say that Jerusalem is the place where men ought to worship." Jesus said to her, "Woman, believe me, the hour is coming when neither on this mountain nor in Jerusalem will you worship the Father. You worship what you do not know; we worship what we know, for salvation is from the Jews. But the hour is coming, and now is, when the true worshipers will worship the Father in spirit and truth, for such the Father seeks to worship him. God is spirit, and those who worship him must worship in spirit and truth." The woman said to him, "I know that the Messiah is coming (he who is called Christ); when he comes, he will show us all things." Jesus said to her, "I who speak to you am he."

Just then his disciples came. They marveled that he was talking with a woman, but none said, "What do you wish?" or, "Why are you talking with her?" So the woman left her water jar, and went away into the city and said to the people, "Come, see a man who told me all that I ever did. Can this be the Christ?" They went out of the city and were coming to him.

Meanwhile the disciples besought him, saying "Rabbi, eat." But he said to them, "I have food to eat of which you do not know." So the disciples said to one another, "Has anyone brought him food?" Jesus said to them, "My food is to do the will of him who sent me, and to accomplish his work. Do not say, 'There are yet four months, then comes the harvest'? I tell you, lift up your eyes, and see how the fields are already white for harvest. He who reaps receives wages, and gathers fruit for eternal life, so that sower and reaper may rejoice together. For here the saying holds true, 'One sow and another reaps.' I sent you to reap that for which you did not labor; others have labored, and you have entered into their labor.''

Many Samaritans from that city believed in him because of the woman's testimony. ''He told me all that I ever did.'' So when the Samaritans came to him, they asked him to stay with them; and he stayed there two days. And many more believed because of his word. They said to the woman, ''It is no longer because of your words that we believe, for we have heard for ourselves, and we know that this is indeed Christ the Savior of the world.''

SUNDAY OF THE BLIND MAN

Verse: You, O Lord, shall keep us and preserve us.
Save me, O Lord,
for the godly man had failed.
The reading is from the Acts of the Apostles.
Chapter 16.16-34.

In those days, as we apostles were going to the place of prayer, we were met by a slave girl who had a spirit of divination and brought her owners much gain by soothsaying. She followed Paul and us, crying, ''These men are servants of the Most High God, who proclaim to you the way of salvation. And this she did for many days. But Paul was annoyed, and turned and said to the spirit, ''I charge you in the name of Jesus Christ to come out of her.'' And it came out that very hour.

But when the owners saw that their hope of gain was gone, they seized Paul and Silas and dragged them into the marketplace before the rulers; and when they

56

had brought them to the magistrates they said, "These men are Jews and they are disturbing our city. They advocate customs which it is not lawful for us Romans to accept or practice." The crowd joined in attacking them; and the magistrates tore the garments off them and gave orders to beat them with rods. And when they had inflicted many blows upon them, they threw them into prison, charging the jailer to keep them safely. Having received this charge, he put them into the inner prison and fastened their feet in the stocks.

But about midnight Paul and Silas were praying and singing hymns to God, and the prisoners were listening to them, and suddenly there was a great earthquake, so that the foundations of the prison were shaken; and immediately all the doors were opened and every one's fetters were unfastened. When the jailer woke and saw that the prison doors were open, he drew his sword and was about to go kill himself, supposing that the prisoners had escaped. But Paul cried our with a loud voice, "Do not harm yourself, for we are all here." And he called for lights and rushed in, and trembling with fear he fell down before Paul and Silas and brought them out and said, "Men, what must I do to be saved?" And they said, "Believe in the Lord Jesus, and you will be saved, you and your household." And they spoke the word of the Lord to him and to all that were in his house. And he took them the same hour of the night, and washed their wounds, and he was baptized at once, with all his family. Then he brought them up into his house, and set food before them; and he rejoiced with all his household that he had believed in God.

57

THE GOSPEL READING
John 9.1-38.

At that time, as Jesus passed by, he saw a man blind from his birth. And his disciples asked him, "Rabbi, who sinned, this man or his parents, that he was born blind?" Jesus answered, "It was not that this man sinned, or his parents, but that the works of God might be made manifest in him. We must work the works of him who sent me, while it is day; night comes, when no one can work. As long as I am in the world, I am the light of the world." As he said this, he spat on the ground and made clay of the spittle and anointed the man's eyes with the clay, saying to him, "Go, wash in the pool of Siloam" (which means Sent). So he went and washed and came back seeing. The neighbors and those who had seen him before as a beggar, said, "Is not this the man who used to sit and beg?" Some said, "It is he"; others said, "No, but he is like him." He said, "I am the man." They said to him, "Then how were your eyes opened?" He answered, "The man called Jesus made clay and anointed my eyes and said to me, 'Go to Siloam and wash'; so I went and washed and received my sight." They said to him, "Where is he?" He said, "I do not know."

They brought to the Pharisees the man who had formerly been blind. Now it was a sabbath day when Jesus made the clay and opened his eyes. The Pharisees again asked him how he had received his sight. And he said to them, "He put clay on my eyes and I wash-ed, and I see." Some of the Pharisees said, "This man is not from God, for he does not keep the sabbath." But others said, "How can a man who is a sinner do such signs?'' There was a division among them. So they again said to the blind man, "What do you say about him, since he has opened your eyes?" He said, "He is a prophet."

The Jews did not believe that he had been blind and had received his sight, until they called the parents of the man who had received his sight, and asked them, "Is this your son, who you say was born blind? How then does he now see?" His parents answered, "We know that this is our son, and that he was born blind; but how he now sees we do not know, nor do we know who opened his eyes. Ask him; he is of age, he will speak for himself." His parents said this because they feared the Jews, for the Jews had already agreed that if anyone should confess him to be Christ he was to be put out of the synagogue. Therefore his parents said, "He is of age, ask him."

So for the second time they called the man who had been blind, and said to him, "Give God the praise; we know that this man is a sinner." He answered, "Whether he is a sinner, I do not know; one thing I know, that though I was blind, now I see." They said to him, "What did he do to you? How did he open your eyes?" He answered them, "I have told you already and you would not listen. Why do you want to hear it again? Do you too want to become his disciples?" And they reviled him, saying, "You are his disciple, but we are disciples of Moses. We know that God has spoken to Moses, but as for this man, we do not know where he comes from." The man answered, "Why, this is a marvel! You do not know where he comes from, and yet he opened my eyes. We know that

God does not listen to sinners, but if anyone is a worshiper of God and does his will, God listens to him. Never since the world began has it been heard that anyone opened the eyes of a man born blind. If this man were not from God, he could do nothing." They answered him, "You were born in utter sin, and would you teach us?" And they cast him out.

Jesus heard that they had cast him out, and having found him he said, "Do you believe in the Son of man?" He answered, "And who is he, sir, that I may believe in him?" Jesus said to him, "You have seen him, and it is he who speaks to you." He said, "Lord, I believe"; and he worshiped him.

SUNDAY OF THE HOLY FATHERS

Verse: Blessed are you, O Lord,
the God of our fathers.
For you are just in all you have done.
The reading is from the Acts of the Apostles.
Chapter 20.16-18; 28-36.
In those days Paul had decided to sail past Ephesos, so that he might not have to spend time in Asia; for he was hastening to be in Jerusalem, if possible, on the day of Pentecost. And from Miletos he sent to Ephesos and called to him the elders of the church. And when they came to him, he said to them: Take heed to yourselves and to all the flock, in which the Holy Spirit has made you guardians, to feed the church of the Lord which he obtained with his own blood. I know that after my departure fierce wolves will come

in among you, not sparing the flock; and from among your own selves will arise men speaking perverse things, to draw away the disciples after them. Therefore be alert, remembering that for three years I did not cease night or day to admonish everyone with tears. And now I commend you to God and to the word of his grace, which is able to build you up and to give you the inheritance among all those who are sanctified. I coveted no one's silver or gold or apparel. You yourselves know that these hands ministered to my necessities, and to those who were with me. In all things I have shown you that by so toiling one must help the weak, remembering the words of the Lord Jesus, how he said, "It is more blessed to give than to receive." And when he had spoken thus, he knelt down and prayed with them all.

THE GOSPEL READING
John 17.1-13.

At that time, Jesus lifted up his eyes to heaven and said, "Father, the hour has come; glorify thy Son that the Son may glorify thee, since thou hast given him power over all flesh, to give eternal life, that they know thee the only true God, and Jesus Christ whom thou hast sent. I glorified thee on earth, having accomplished the work which thou gavest me to do; and now, Father glorify thou me in thy own presence with the glory which I had with thee before the world was made.

"I have manifested thy name to the men whom thou gavest me out of the world; thine they were, and thou gavest them to me, and they have kept thy word. Now they know that everything that thou hast given me is from thee; for I have given them the words which thou gavest me, and they have received them and know in truth that I came from thee; and they have believed that thou didst send me. I am praying for them; I am not praying for the world but for those whom thou hast given me, for they are thine; all mine are thine, and thine are mine, and I am glorified in them. And now I am no more in the world, but they are in the world, and I am coming to thee. Holy Father, keep them in thy name, which thou has given me, that they may be one, even as we are one. While I was with them, I kept them in thy name, which thou hast given me; I have guarded them, and none of them is lost but the son of perdition, that the scripture might be fulfilled. But now I am coming to thee; and these things I speak in the world, that they may have my joy fulfilled in themselves."

SUNDAY OF PENTECOST

Verse: Their voice has gone out into all the earth.
The heavens declare the glory of God.
The reading is from the Acts of the Apostles.
Chapter 2.1-11.
When the day of Pentecost has come, they were all together in one place. And suddenly a sound came from heaven like the rush of a mighty wind, and it filled all the house where they were sitting. And there appeared to them tongues as of fire, distributed and

resting on each one of them. And they were all filled with the Holy Spirit and began to speak in other tongues, as the Spirit gave them utterance.

Now there were dwelling in Jerusalem Jews, devout men from every nation under heaven. And at this sound the multitude came together, and they were bewildered, because each one heard them speaking in his own language. And they were amazed and wondered, saying, "Are not all these who are speaking Galileans? And how is it that we hear, each of us in his own native language? Parthians and Medes and Elamites and residents of Mesopotamia, Judea and Cappadocia, Pontos and Asia, Phrygia and Pamphylia, Egypt and the parts of Libya belonging to Cyrene, and visitors from Rome, both Jews and proselytes, Cretans and Arabians, we hear them telling in their own tongues the mighty works of God."

THE GOSPEL READING
John 7.37-52.

On the last day of the feast, the great day, Jesus stood up and proclaimed, "If any one thirst, let him come to me and drink. He who believes in me, as the scripture has said, 'Out of his heart shall flow rivers of living water.' Now this he said about the Spirit, which those who believed in him were to receive; for as yet the Spirit had not been given, because Jesus was not yet glorified.

When they heard these words, some of the people said, "This is really the prophet." Others said, "This is the Christ." But some said, "Is the Christ to come from Galilee? Has not the scripture said that the Christ is descended from David, and comes from Bethlehem, the village where David was?'' So there was a division among the people over him. Some of them wanted to arrest him, but no one laid hands on him.

The officers then went back to the chief priest and Pharisees, who said to them, ''Why did you not bring him?'' The officers answered, ''No man ever spoke like this man!'' The Pharisees answered them, ''Are you led astray, you also? Have any of the authorities or of the Pharisees believed in him? But this crowd, who do not know the law, are accursed.'' Nicodemos, who had gone to him before, and who was one of them, said to them, ''Does our law judge a man without first giving him a hearing and learning what he does?'' They replied, ''Are you from Galilee too? Search and you will see that no prophet is to rise from Galilee.''

SUNDAY OF ALL SAINTS

Verse: God is wonderful among his saints.
Bless God in the congregations.
The reading is from Paul's Letter to the Hebrews.
Chapters 11.33-40; 12.1-2.
Brethren, the saints through faith conquered kingdoms, enforced justice, received promises, stopped the mouths of lions, quenched raging fire, escaped the edge of the sword, won strength out of weakness, became mighty in war, put foreign armies to fight. Women received their dead by resurrection. Some were

64

tortured, refusing to accept release, that they might rise again to a better life. Others suffered mocking and scourging, and even chains and imprisonment. They were stoned, they were sawn in two, they were killed with the sword; they went about in skins of sheep and goats, destitute, afflicted, ill-treated (of whom the world was not worthy) wandering over deserts and mountains, and in dens and caves of the earth. And all these, though well attested by their faith, did nor receive what was promised, since God had forseen something better for us, that apart from us they should not be made perfect.

THE GOSPEL READING
Matthew 10.32-33, 37-38; 19.27-30.

The Lord said to his disciples, "Everyone who acknowledges me before men, I also will acknowledge him before my Father who is in heaven; but whoever denies me before men, I also will deny him before my Father who is in heaven.

"He who loves father or mother more than me is not worthy of me; and he who does not take his cross and follow me is not worthy of me." Then Peter said in reply, "Lo, we have left everything and followed you. What then shall we have?" Jesus said to them, "Truly, I say to you, in the new world, when the Son of man shall sit on his glorious throne, you who have followed me will also sit on twelve thrones, judging the twelve tribes of Israel. And everyone who has left houses or brothers or sisters or father or mother or children or lands, for my name's sake, will receive a

65

hundredfold, and inherit eternal life. But many that are first will be last, and the last first.''

SECOND SUNDAY

Verse: Let your mercy, O Lord, be upon us.
Rejoice in the Lord, O you righteous.
The reading is from Paul's Letter to the Romans.
Chapter 2.10-16.

Brethren, glory and honor and peace for everyone who does good, the Jew first and also the Greek. For God shows no partiality.

All who have sinned without the law will also perish without the law, and all who have sinned under the law will be judged by the law. For it is not the hearers of the law who are righteous before God, but the doers of the law who will be justified. When Gentiles who have not the law do by nature what the law requires, they are a law to themselves, even though they do not have the law. They show that what the law requires is written on their hearts, while their conscience also bears witness and their conflicting thoughts accuse or excuse them on that day when, according to my gospel, God judges the secrets of men by Christ Jesus.

THE GOSPEL READING
Matthew 4.18-23.

At that time, Jesus walked by the Sea of Galilee, he saw two brothers, Simon who is called Peter and Andrew his brother, casting a net into the sea; for they were fishermen. And he said to them, "Follow me, and I will make you fishers of men." Immediately they left their nets and followed him. And going on from there he saw two other brothers, James the son of Zebedee and John his brother, in the boat with Zebedee their father, mending their nets, and he called them. Immediately they left the boat and their father, and followed him.

And he went about all Galilee, teaching in their synagogues and preaching the gospel of the kingdom and healing every disease and every infirmity among the people.

THIRD SUNDAY

Verse: The Lord is my strength and my song.
The Lord has chastened me sorely.
The reading is from Paul's Letter to the Romans.
Chapter 5.1-11.

Brethren, since we are justified by faith, we have peace with God through our Lord Jesus Christ. Through him we have obtained access to this grace in which we stand, and we rejoice in our hope of sharing the glory of God. More than that, we rejoice in our sufferings, knowing that suffering produces endurance, and endurance produces character, and character produces hope, and hope does not disappoint us, because God's love has been poured into our hearts through the Holy Spirit which has been given to us.

While we were still weak, at the right time Christ died for the ungodly. Why, one will hardly die for a righteous man—though perhaps for a good man one will dare even to die. But God shows his love for us in that while we were yet sinners Christ died for us. Since, therefore, we are now justified by his blood, much more shall we be saved by him from the wrath of God. For if while we were enemies we were reconciled to God by the death of his Son, much more, now that we are reconciled, shall we be saved by his life.

THE GOSPEL READING
Matthew 6.22-33.

The Lord said: "The eye is the lamp of the body. So, if your eye is sound, your whole body will be full of light; but if your eye is not sound, your whole body will be full of darkness. If then the light in you is darkness, how great is the darkness!

"No one can serve two masters; for either he will hate the one and love the other, or he will be devoted to the one and despise the other. You cannot serve God and mammon.

"Therefore I tell you, do not be anxious about your life, what you shall eat or what you shall drink, nor about your body, what you shall put on. Is not life more than food, and the body more than clothing? Look at the birds of the air: they neither sow nor reap nor gather into barns, and yet your heavenly Father feeds them. Are you not of more value than they? And which of you by being anxious can add one cubit to his span of life? And why are you anxious about clothing? Consider the lilies of the field, how they grow; they neither toil nor spin; yet I tell you, even

Solomon in all his glory was not arrayed like one of these. But if God so clothes the grass of the field, which today is alive and tomorrow is thrown into the oven, will he not much more clothe you, O men of little faith? Therefore do not be anxious, saying 'What shall we drink?' or 'What shall we wear?' For the Gentiles seek all these things; and your heavenly Father knows that you need them all. But seek first his kingdom and his righteousness, and all these things shall be yours as well.''

FOURTH SUNDAY

Verse: Sing praises to our God, sing praises.
Clap your hands, all you nations.
The reading is from Paul's Letter to the Romans.
Chapter 6.18-23.
Brethren, having been set free from sin, you have become slaves of righteousness. I am speaking in human terms, because of your natural limitations. For just as you once yielded your members to impurity and to greater and greater iniquity, so now yield your members to righteousness for sanctification.

When you were slaves of sin, you were free in regard to righteousness. But then what return did you get from the things of which you are now ashamed? The end of those things is death. But now that you have been set free from sin and have become slaves of God, the return you get is sanctification and its end, eternal life. For the wages of sin is death, but the free gift of God is eternal life in Christ Jesus our Lord.

THE GOSPEL READING
Matthew 8.5-13.

At that time, as Jesus entered Capernaum, a centurion came forward to him, beseeching him and saying, "Lord, my servant is lying paralyzed at home, in terrible distress." And he said to him, "I will come and heal him." But the centurion answered him, "Lord, I am not worthy to have you come under my roof; but only say the word, and my servant will be healed. For I am a man under authority, with soldiers under me; and I say to one, 'Go,' and he goes, and to another, 'Come,' and he comes, and to my slave, 'Do this,' and he does it." When Jesus heard him, he marveled, and said to those who followed him, "Truly, I say to you, not even in Israel have I found such faith. I tell you, many will come from east and west and sit at table with Abraham, Isaac, and Jacob in the kingdom of heaven, while the sons of the kingdom will be thrown into the outer darkness; there men will weep and gnash their teeth." And to the centurion Jesus said, "Go; be it done for you as you have believed." And the servant was healed at that very moment.

FIFTH SUNDAY

Verse: O Lord, how magnificent are your works.
You have made all things in wisdom.
Bless the Lord, O my soul.
The reading is from Paul's Letter to the Romans.
Chapter 10.1-10.
Brethren, my heart's desire and prayer to God for

70

them is that they may be saved. I bear them witness that they have a zeal for God, but it is not enlightened. For, being ignorant of the righteousness that comes from God and seeking to establish their own, they did not submit to God's righteousness. For Christ is the end of the law, that everyone who has faith may be justified.

Moses writes that the man who practices the righteousness which is based on the law shall live by it. But the righteousness based on faith says, Do not say in your heart, "Who will ascend into heaven?" (that is, to bring Christ down) or "Who will descend into the abyss?" (that is, to bring Christ up from the dead). But what does it say? The word is near you, on your lips and in your heart (that is, the word of faith which we preach); because, if you confess with your lips that Jesus is Lord and believe in your heart that God raised him from the dead, you will be saved. For man believes with his heart and so is justified, and he confesses with his lips and so is saved.

THE GOSPEL READING
Matthew 8.28-34; 9.1

At that time, when Jesus came to the other side, to the country of the Gadarenes, two demoniancs met him, coming out of the tombs, so fierce that no one could pass that way. And behold, they cried out, "What have you to do with us, O Son of God? Have you come here to torment us before the time?" Now a herd of many swine was feeding at some distance from them. And the demons begged him, "If you cast

71

us out, send us away into the herd of swine." And he said to them, "Go." So they came out and went into the swine; and behold, the whole herd rushed down the steep bank into the sea, and perished in the waters. The herdsmen fled, and going into the city they told everything, and what had happened to the demoniacs. And behold, all the city came out to meet Jesus; and when they saw him, they begged him to leave their neighborhood.

And getting into a boat he crossed over and came to his own city.

SIXTH SUNDAY

Verse: You, O Lord, shall keep us and preserve us.
Save me, O Lord,
for the godly man has failed.
The reading is from Paul's Letter to the Romans.
Chapter 12.6-14.

Brethren, having gifts that differ according to the grace given to us, let us use them; if prophecy, in proportion to our faith; if service, in our serving; he who teaches, in his teaching; he who exhorts, in his exhortation; he who contributes, in liberality; he who gives aid, with zeal; he who does acts of mercy, with cheerfulness.

Let love be genuine; hate what is evil, hold fast to what is good; love one another with brotherly affection; outdo one another in showing honor. Never flag in zeal, be aglow with the spirit, serve the Lord. Rejoice in your hope, be patient in tribulation, be constant in prayer. Contribute to the needs of the saints, practice hospitality.

Bless those who persecute you; bless and do not curse them.

THE GOSPEL READING
Matthew 9.1-8.

At that time, getting into a boat Jesus crossed over and came to his own city. And behold, they brought to him a paralytic, lying on his bed; and when Jesus saw their faith he said to the paralytic, "Take heart, my son; your sins are forgiven." And behold, some of the scribes said to themselves, "This man is blaspheming." But Jesus knowing their thoughts, said, "Why do you think evil in your hearts? For which is easier, to say 'Your sins are forgiven,' or to say 'Rise and walk?' But that you may know that the Son of man has authority on earth to forgive sins"—he then said to the paralytic—"Rise, take up your bed and go home." And he rose and went home. When the crowds saw it, they were afraid, and they glorified God, who had given such authority to men.

SEVENTH SUNDAY

Verse: O Lord, save your people
and bless your inheritance.
To you, O Lord, have I cried, O my God.
The reading is from Paul's Letter to the Romans.
Chapter 15.1-7.

73

Brethren, we who are strong ought to bear with the failings of the weak, and not to please ourselves; let each of us please his neighbor for his good, to edify him. For Christ did not please himself; but, as it is written, "The reproaches of those who reproached thee fell on me." For whatever was written in former days was written for our instruction, that by steadfastness and by the encouragement of the scriptures we might have hope. May the God of steadfastness and encouragement grant you to live in such harmony with one another, in accord with Christ Jesus, that together you may with one voice glorify the God and Father of our Lord Jesus Christ.

Welcome one another, therefore, as Christ has welcomed you, for the glory of God.

THE GOSPEL READING
Matthew 9.27-35.

At that time, as Jesus passed on from there, two blind men followed him, crying aloud, "Have mercy on us, Son of David." When he entered the house, the blind men came to him, and Jesus said to them, "Do you believe that I am able to do this?" They said to him, "Yes, Lord." Then he touched their eyes, saying, "According to your faith be it done to you." And their eyes were opened. And Jesus sternly charged them, "See that no one knows it." But they went away and spread his fame through all that district.

As they were going away, behold, a dumb demoniac was brought to him. And when the demon had been cast out, the dumb man spoke; and the crowds marveled, saying, "Never was anything like this seen in Israel." But the Pharisees said, "He casts out demons by the prince of demons."

And Jesus went about all the cities and villages, teaching in their synagogues and preaching the gospel of the kingdom, and healing every disease and every infirmity among people.

EIGHTH SUNDAY

Verse: The Lord will give strength to his people.
Bring to the Lord, O Son of God,
bring to the Lord honor and glory.
The reading is from Paul's First Letter to the
Corinthians.
Chapter 1.10-17.
Brethren, I appeal to you, by the name of our Lord Jesus Christ, that all of you agree and that there be no dissensions among you, but that you be united in the same mind and the same judgment. For it has been reported to me by Chloe's people that there is quarrelling among you, my brethren. What I mean is that each one of you says, "I belong to Paul," or "I belong to Apollos," or "I belong to Cephas," or "I belong to Christ." Is Christ divided? Was Paul crucified for you? Or were you baptized in the name of Paul? I am thankful that I baptized none of you except Crispus and Gaius; lest anyone should say that you were baptized in my name. (I did baptize also the household of Stephanas. Beyond that, I do not know whether I

baptized anyone else.) For Christ did not send me to baptize but to preach the gospel, and not with eloquent wisdom, lest the cross of Christ be emptied of its power.

For the word of the cross is folly to those who are perishing, but to us who are being saved it is the power of God.

THE GOSPEL READING
Matthew 14.14-22.

At that time, Jesus saw a great throng; and he had compassion on them, and healed their sick. When it was evening, the disciples came to him and said, "This is a lonely place, and the day is now over; send the crowds away to go into the villages and buy food for themselves." Jesus said, "They need not go away; you give them something to eat." They said to him, "We have only five loaves here and two fish." And he said, "Bring them here to me." Then he ordered the crowds to sit down on the grass; and taking the five loaves and the two fish he looked up to heaven, and blessed, and broke and gave the loaves to the crowds. And they all ate and were satisfied. And they took up twelve baskets full of the broken pieces left over. And those who ate were about five thousand men, besides women and children.

Then he made the disciples get into the boat and go before him to the other side, while he dismissed the crowds.

NINTH SUNDAY

Verse: Make your vows to the Lord our God
and perform them.
God is known in Judah;
his name is great in Israel.
The reading is from Paul's First Letter to the
Corinthians.
Chapter 3.9-17.

Brethren, we are God's fellow workers; you are God's field, God's building.

According to the grace of God given to me, like a skilled master builder I laid a foundation, and another man is building upon it. Let each man take care how he builds upon it. For no other foundation can anyone lay than that which is laid, which is Jesus Christ. Now if anyone builds on the foundation with gold, silver, precious stones, wood, hay, straw—each man's work will become manifest; for the Day will disclose it, because it will be revealed with fire, and the fire will test what sort of work each one has done. If the work which any man has built on the foundation survives, he will receive a reward. If any man's work is burned up, he will suffer loss, though he himself will be saved, but only as through fire.

Do you not know that you are God's temple and that God's spirit dwells in you? If anyone destroys God's temple, God will destroy him. For God's temple is holy, and that temple you are.

THE GOSPEL READING
Matthew 14.22-34.

At that time, Jesus made the disciples get into the boat and go before him to the other side, while he dismissed the crowds. And after he had dismissed the crowds, he went up into the hills by himself to pray. When evening came, he was there alone, but the boat by this time was many furlongs distant from the land, beaten by the waves; for the wind was against them. And in the fourth watch of the night he came to them, walking on the sea. But when the disciples saw him walking on the sea, they were terrified, saying, "It is a ghost!" And they cried out for fear. But immediately he spoke to them, saying "Take heart, it is I; have no fear."

And Peter answered him, "Lord, if it is you, bid me come to you on the water." He said, "Come." So Peter got out of the boat and walked on the water and came to Jesus; but when he saw the wind, he was afraid, and beginning to sink he cried out, "Lord, save me." Jesus immediately reached out his hand and caught him, saying to him, "O man of little faith, why did you doubt?" And when they got into the boat, the wind ceased. And those in the boat worshiped him, saying, "Truly you are the Son of God."

And when they had crossed over, they came to land at Gennesaret.

TENTH SUNDAY

Verse: Let your mercy, O Lord, be upon us,
Rejoice in the Lord, O you righteous.
The reading is from Paul's First Letter to the
Corinthians.
Chapter 4.9-16.

Brethren, God has exhibited us apostles as last of all, like men sentenced to death; because we have become a spectacle to the world, to angels and to men. We are fools for Christ's sake, but you are wise in Christ. We are weak, but you are strong. You are held in honor, but we in disrepute. To the present hour we hunger and thirst, we are ill-clad and buffeted and homeless, and we labor, working with our own hands. When reviled, we bless; when persecuted, we endure; when slandered, we try to conciliate; we have become, and are now, as the refuse of the world, the offscouring of all things.

I do not write this to make you ashamed, but to admonish you as my beloved children. For though you have countless guides in Christ, you do not have many fathers. For I became your father in Christ Jesus through the gospel. I urge you, then, be imitators of me.

THE GOSPEL READING
Matthew 17.14-23.

At that time, a man came up to him and kneeling before him said, "Lord, have mercy on my son, for he is an epileptic and he suffers terribly; for often he falls into the fire, and often into the water. And I brought him to your disciples, and they could not heal him." And Jesus answered, "O faithless and perverse generation, how long am I to be with you? Bring him here to me." And Jesus rebuked him, and the demon came out of him, and the boy was cured instantly. Then the disciples came to Jesus privately and said, "Why could we not cast it out?" He said to them, "Because of your little faith. For truly I say to you, if you have faith as a grain of mustard seed, you will saw to this mountain, 'Move hence to yonder place,' and it will move; and nothing will be impossible to you."

As they were gathering in Galilee, Jesus said to them, "The Son of man is to be delivered into the hands of men, and they will kill him, and he will be raised on the third day."

ELEVENTH SUNDAY

Verse: The Lord is my strength and my song.
The Lord has chastened me sorely.
The reading is from Paul's First Letter to the Corinthians.
Chapter 9.2-12.
Brethren, you are the seal of my apostleship in the Lord. This is my defense to those who would examine me. Do we not have the right to our food and drink? Do we not have the right to be accompanied by a wife, as the other apostles and the brethren of the Lord and Cephas? Or is it only Barnabas and I who have no right to refrain from working for a living? Who serves as

a soldier at his own expense? Who plants a vineyard without eating any of its fruit? Do I say this on human authority? Does not the Lord say the same? For it is written in the law of Moses, "You shall not muzzle an ox when it is treading out the grain." Is it for oxen that God is concerned? Does he not speak entirely for our sake? It was written for our sake, because the plowman should plow in hope and the thresher thresh in hope of a share in the crop. If we have sown spiritual good among you, is it too much if we reap your material benefits? If others share this rightful claim upon you, do not we still more? Nevertheless, we have not made use of this right, but we endure anything rather than put an obstacle in the way of the gospel of Christ.

THE GOSPEL READING
Matthew 18.23-35.

The Lord said this parable: "The kingdom of heaven may be compared to a king who wished to settle accounts with his servants. When he began the reckoning, one was brought to him who owed him ten thousand talents; and as he could not pay, his lord ordered him to be sold, with his wife and children and all that he had, and payment to be made. So the servant fell on his knees, imploring him, 'Lord, have patience with me, and I will pay you everything.' And out of pity for him the lord of that servant released him and forgave him the debt. But that same servant, as he went out, came upon one of his fellow servants who owed him a hundred denarii; and seizing him by the throat he said, 'Pay what you owe.' So his fellow servant fell down and besought him, 'Have patience with me, and I will pay you.' He refused and went and put him in prison till he should pay the debt. When his fellow servants saw what had taken place, they were greatly distressed, and they went and reported to their lord all that had taken place. Then his lord summoned him and said to him, 'You wicked servant! I forgave you all that debt because you besought me; and should not you have had mercy on your fellow servant, as I had mercy on you?' And in anger his lord delivered his to the jailers, till he should pay all his debt. So also my heavenly Father will do to everyone of you if you do not forgive your brother from your heart.''

TWELFTH SUNDAY

Verse: Sing praises to our God, sing praises.
Clap your hands, all you nations.
The reading is from Paul's First Letter to the
Corinthians.
Chapter 15.1-11..

Brethren, I would remind you in what terms I preached to you the gospel, which you received, in which you stand, by which you are saved, if you hold it fast—unless you believed in vain.

For I delivered to you as of first importance what I also received, that Christ died for our sins in accordance with the scriptures, that he was buried, that he was raised on the third day in accordance with the scriptures, and that he appeared to Cephas, then to the twelve. Then he appeared to more than five hundred brethren at one time, most of whom are still alive, though some have fallen asleep. Then he appeard to James, then to all the apostles. Last of all, as to one untimely born, he appeared also to me. For I am the least of the apostles, unfit to be called an apostle, because I persecuted the church of God. But by the grace of God I am what I am, and his grace toward me was not in vain. On the contrary, I worked harder than any of them, though it was not I, but the grace of God which is with me. Whether then it was I or they, so we preach and so you believed.

THE GOSPEL READING
Matthew 19.16-24.

At that time, a young man came up to Jesus, kneeling and saying, "Good Teacher, what good deed must I do, to have eternal life?" And he said to him, "Why do you call me good? One there is who is good. If you would enter life, keep the commandments." He said to him, "Which?" And Jesus said, "You shall not kill, You shall not commit adultery, You shall not steal, You shall not bear false witness, Honor your father and mother, and You shall love your neighbor as yourself." The young man said to him, "All these I have observed; what do I still lack?" Jesus said to him, "If you would be perfect, go, sell what you possess and give to the poor, and you will have treasure in heaven; and come, follow me." When the young man heard this he went away sorrowful; for he had great possessions.

And Jesus said to his disciples, "Truly, I say to you, it will be hard for a rich man to enter the kingdom of heaven. Again I tell you, it is easier for a camel to go through the eye of a needle than for a rich man to enter the kingdom of God." When the disciples heard this they were greatly astonished, saying, "Who then can be saved?" But Jesus looked at them and said to them, "With men this is impossible, but with God all things are possible."

THIRTEENTH SUNDAY

Verse: O Lord, how magnificent are your works.
You have made all things in wisdom.
Bless the Lord, O my soul.
The reading is from Paul's First Letter to the
Corinthians.
Chapter 16.13-24.
Brethren, be watchful, stand firm in your faith, be courageous, be strong. Let all that you do be done in love.

Now, brethren, you know that the household of Stephanas were the first converts in Achaia, and they have devoted themselves to the service of the saints; I urge you to be subject to such men and to every fellow worker and laborer. I rejoice at the coming of Stephanas and Fortunatus and Achaicus, because they have made up for your absence; for they refreshed my spirit as well as yours. Give recognition to such men.

The churches of Asia send greetings. Aquila and Prisca, together with the church in their house, send you hearty greetings in the Lord. All the brethren send greetings. Greet one another with a holy kiss.

I, Paul, write this greeting with my own hand. If any one has no love for the Lord, let him be accursed. Our Lord, come! The grace of the Lord Jesus be with you. My love be with you all in Christ Jesus. Amen.

THE GOSPEL READING
Matthew 21.33-42.

The Lord said this parable: "There was a householder who planted a vineyard, and set a hedge around it, and dug a wine press in it, and built a tower, and let it out to tenants, and went into another country. When the season of fruit drew near, he sent his servants to the tenants, to get his fruit; and the tenants took his servants and beat one, killed another, and stoned another. Again he sent other servants, more than the first; and they did the same to them. Afterward he sent his son to them, saying 'They will respect my son.' But when the tenants saw the son, they said to themselves, 'This is the heir; come, let us kill him and have his inheritance.' And they took him and cast him out of the vineyard and killed him. When therefore the owner of the vineyard comes, what will he do to those tenants?" They said to him, "He will put those wretches to a miserable death, and let out the vineyard to other tenants who will give him the fruits in their seasons."

Jesus said to them, "Have you never read in the scriptures:

'The very stone which the builders rejected has

has become the head of the corner; this was the Lord's doing, and it is marvelous in our eyes?' "

FOURTEENTH SUNDAY

Verse: You, O Lord, shall keep us and preserve us.
Save me, O Lord,
for the godly man has failed.
The reading is from Paul's Second Letter to the
Corinthians.
Chapters 1.21-24; 2.1-4.

Brethren, it is God who establishes us with you in Christ, and has commissioned us; he has put his seal upon us and given us his Spirit in our hearts as a guarantee.

But I call God to witness against me—it was to spare you that I refrained from coming to Corinth. Not that we lord it over our faith; we work with you for your joy, for you stand firm in your faith. For I made up my mind not to make you another painful visit. For if I cause you pain, who is there to make me glad but the one whom I have pained? And I wrote as I did, so that when I came I might not suffer pain from those who should have made me rejoice, for I felt sure of all of you, that my joy would be the joy of you all. For I wrote you out of much affliction and anguish of heart and with many tears, not to cause you pain but to let you know the abundant love that I have for you.

THE GOSPEL READING
Matthew 22.2-14.

The Lord said this parable: "The kingdom of heaven may be compared to a king who gave a marriage feast for his son, and sent his servants to call those who were invited to the marriage feast; but they would not come. Again he sent other servants, saying, 'Tell those who are invited, Behold, I have made ready my dinner, my oxen and my fat calves are killed, and everything is ready; come to the marriage feast.' But they made light of it and went off, one to his farm, another to his business, while the rest seized his servants, treated them shamefully, and killed them. The king was angry, and sent his troops and destroyed those murderers and burned their city. Then he said to his servants, 'The wedding is ready, but those invited were not worthy. Go therefore to the thoroughfares, and invite to the marriage feast as many as you find.' And those servants went out into the streets and gathered all whom they found, both bad and good; so the wedding hall was filled with guests.

"But when the king came in to look at the guests, he saw there a man who had no wedding garment; and he said to him, 'Friend, how did you get in here without a wedding garment?' And he was speechless. Then the king said to the attendants, 'Bind him hand and foot, and cast him into the outer darkness; there men will weep and gnash their teeth.' For many are called, but few are chosen."

FIFTEENTH SUNDAY

Verse: O Lord, save your people
and bless your inheritance.
To you, O Lord, have I cried, O my God.
The reading is from Paul's Second Letter to the
Corinthians.
Chapter 4.6-15.

Brethren, it is God who said, "Let light shine out
of darkness," who has shone in our hearts to give the
light of the knowledge of the glory of God in the face
of Christ.

But we have this treasure in earthen vessels, to show
that the transcendent power belongs to God and not
to us. We are afflicted in every way, but not crushed;
perplexed, but not driven to despair; persecuted, but
not forsaken; struck down, but not destroyed; always
carrying in the body the death of Jesus, so that the
life of Jesus may also be manifested in our bodies. For
while we live we are always being given up to death
for Jesus' sake, so that the life of Jesus may be
manifested in our mortal flesh. So death is at work
in us but life in you.

Since we have the same spirit of faith as he had who
wrote, "I believed, and so I spoke," we too believe,
and so we speak, knowing that he who raised the Lord
Jesus will raise us also with Jesus and bring us with
you into his presence. For it is all for your sake, so
that as grace extends to more and more people it may
increase thanksgiving, to the glory of God.

THE GOSPEL READING
Matthew 22.35-46.

At that time a lawyer, asked him a question, to test him. "Teacher, which is the great commandment in the law?" And he said to him, "You shall love the Lord your God with all your heart, and with all your soul, and with all your mind. This is the great and first commandment. And a second is like it, You shall love your neighbor as yourself. On these two command- ments depend all the law and the prophets."

Now while the Pharisees were gathered together, Jesus asked them a question, saying "What do you think of Christ? Whose son is he?" They said to him, "The son of David." He said to them, "How is it then that David, inspired by the Spirit, calls him Lord, saying,

'The Lord said to my Lord,

Sit at my right hand,

till I put thy enemies under thy feet'?

If David thus calls him Lord, how is he his son?" And no one was able to answer him a word, nor from that day did anyone dare to ask him any more questions.

SIXTEENTH SUNDAY

Verse: The Lord will give strength to his people.
Bring to the Lord, O sons of God,
bring to the Lord honor and glory.
The reading is from Paul's Second Letter to the Corinthians.

Chapter 6.1-10.

Brethren, working together with him, we entreat you not to accept the grace of God in vain. For he says, "At the acceptable time I have listened to you, and helped you on the day of salvation." Behold, now is the acceptable time; behold, now is the day of salvation. We put no obstacle in anyone's way, so that no fault may be found with our ministry, but as servants of God we commend ourselves in every way: through great endurance, in afflictions, hardships, calamities, beatings, imprisonments, tumults, labors, watching, hunger; by purity, knowledge, forbearance, kindness, the Holy Spirit, genuine love, truthful speech, and the power of God; with the weapons of righteousness for the right hand and for the left; in honor and dishonor, in ill repute and good repute. We are treated as imposters, and yet are true; as unknown, and yet well-known; as dying, and behold we live; as punished, and yet not killed; as sorrowful, yet always rejoicing; as poor, yet making many rich; as having nothing, and yet possessing everything.

THE GOSPEL READING
Matthew 25.14-30

The Lord said this parable: "A man going on a journey called his servants and entrusted to them his property; to one he gave five talents, to another two, to another one, to each according to his ability. Then he went away. He who had received the five talents went at once and traded with them; and he made five talents more. So also, he who had the two talents made two talents more. But he who had received the one talent went and dug in the ground and hid his master's money. Now after a long time the master of those servants came and settled accounts with them. And he who had received the five talents came forward, bringing five talents more, saying, 'Master, you delivered to me five talents; here I have made five talents more.' His master said to him, 'Well done, good and faithful servant; you have been faithful over a little, I will set you over much; enter into the joy of your master.' And he also who had the two talents came forward, saying, 'Master, you delivered to me two talents; here I have made two talents more.' His master said to him, 'Well done, good and faithful servant; you have been faithful over a little, I will set you over much; enter into the joy of your master.' He also who had received the one talent came forward, saying, 'Master, I knew you to be a hard man, reaping where you did not sow, and gathering where you did not winnow; so I was afraid, and I went and hid your talent in the ground. Here you have what is yours.' But his master answered him, 'You wicked and slothful servant! You knew that I reap where I have not sowed and gather where I have not winnowed? Then you ought to have invested my money with the bankers and at my coming I should have received what was my own with interest. So take the talent from him, and give it to him who has the ten talents. For to every one who has will more be given, and he will have abundance; but from him who has not, even what he has will be taken away. And cast the worthless servant into the outer darkness; there men will weap and gnash their teeth.' As he said these things he cried out: "He who has ears to hear, let him hear!"

SEVENTEENTH SUNDAY

Verse: Make your vows to the Lord our God
and perform them.
God is known in Judah;
his name is great in Israel.
The reading is from Paul's Second Letter to the
Corinthians.
Chapters 6.16-18; 7.1

Brethren, what agreement has the temple of God
with idols? For we are the temple of the living God;
as God said,

"I will live in them and move among them
and I will be their God,
and they shall be my people.
Therefore come out from them and be separate
from them, says the Lord,
and touch nothing unclean;
then I will welcome you,
and I will be a father to you,
and you shall be my sons and daughters,
says the Lord Almighty."

Since we have these promises, beloved, let us cleanse
ourselves from every defilement of body and spirit,
and make holiness perfect in the fear of God.

Open your hearts to us; we have wronged no one,
we have corrupted no one, we have taken advantage
of no one.

THE GOSPEL READING
Matthew 15.21-28.

At that time, Jesus went to the district of Tyre and Sidon. And behold, a Canaanite woman from that region came out and cried, "Have mercy on me, O Lord, Son of David; my daughter is severely possessed by a demon." But he did not answer her a word. And his disciples came and begged him, saying, "Send her away, for she is crying after us." He answered, "I was sent only to the lost sheep of the house of Israel." But she came and knelt before him, saying, "Lord, help me." And he answered, "It is not fair to take the children's bread and throw it to the dogs." She said, "Yes, Lord, yet even the dogs eat the crumbs that fall from their master's table." Then Jesus answered her, "O woman, great is your faith! Be it done for you as you desire." And her daughter was healed instantly.

EIGHTEENTH SUNDAY

Verse: Let your mercy, O Lord, be upon us,
Rejoice in the Lord, O you righteous.
The reading is from Paul's Second Letter to the
Corinthians.
Chapter 9.6-11.

Brethren, the point is this: he who sows sparingly will also reap sparingly, and he who sows bountifully will also reap bountifully. Each one must do as he has made up his mind, not reluctantly or under compulsion, for God loves a cheerful giver. And God is able to provide you with every blessing in abundance, so that you may always have enough of everything and may provide in abundance for every good work. As it is written,

"He scatters abroad, he gives to the poor;
his righteousness endures forever."

He who supplies seed to the sower and bread for food will supply and multiply your resources and increase the harvest of your righteousness. You will be enriched in every way for great generosity, which through us will produce thanksgiving to God.

THE GOSPEL READING
Luke 5.1-11.

At that time Jesus was standing by the lake of Gennesaret. And he saw two boats by the lake; but the fishermen had gone out of them and were washing their nets. Getting into one of the boats, which was Simon's, he asked him to put out a little from the land. And he sat down and taught the people from the boat. And when he had ceased speaking, he said to Simon, "Put out into the deep and let down your nets for a catch." And Simon answered, "Master, we toiled all night and took nothing! But at your word I will let down the nets." And when they had done this, they enclosed a great shoal of fish; and as their nets were breaking, they beckoned to their partners in the other boat to come and help them. And they came and filled both the boats, so that they began to sink. But when Simon Peter saw it, he fell down at Jesus' knees, saying, "Depart from me, for I am a sinful man, O Lord." For he was astonished, and all that were with him, at the catch of fish which they had taken; and so also were James and John, sons of Zebedee, who were partners with Simon. And Jesus said to Simon, "Do not be afraid; henceforth you will be catching men." And when they had brought their boats to land, they left everything and followed him.

NINETEENTH SUNDAY

Verse: The Lord is my strength and my song.
The Lord has chastened me sorely.
The reading is from Paul's Second Letter to the Corinthians.
Chapters 11.31-33; 12.1-9.

Brethren, the God and Father of the Lord Jesus, he who is blessed for ever, knows that I do not lie. At Damascus, the governor under King Aretas guarded the city of Damascus in order to seize me, but I was let down in a basket through a window in the wall, and escaped his hands. I must boast; there is nothing to be gained by it, but I will go on to visions and revelations of the Lord. I know a man in Christ who fourteen years ago was caught up to the third heaven—whether in the body or out of the body I do not know, God knows. And I know that this man was caught up into paradise—whether in the body or out of the body I do not know, God knows—and he heard things that cannot be told, which man may not utter. On behalf of this man I will boast, but on my own behalf I will not boast, except of my weaknesses. Though if I wish to boast, I shall not be a fool, for I shall be speaking the truth. But I refrain from it, so that no one may think more of me than he sees in me or hears from me. And to keep me from being too elated by the abundance of revelations, a thorn was given me in the flesh, a messenger of Satan, to harass me, to keep me from being too elated. Three times I besought the Lord about this, that it should leave me; but he said to me, "My grace is sufficient for you, for my power is made perfect in weakness." I will all the more gladly boast of my weaknesses, that the power of Christ may rest upon me.

THE GOSPEL READING
Luke 6.31-36.

The Lord said: "As you wish that men would do to you, do so to them.

"If you love those who love you, what credit is that to you? For even sinners love those who love them. And if you do good to those who do good to you, what credit is that to you? For even sinners do the same. And if you lend to those from whom you hope to receive, what credit is that to you? Even sinners lend to sinners, to receive as much again. But love your enemies, and do good, and lend, expecting nothing in return; and your reward will be great, and you will be sons of the Most High; for he is kind to the ungrateful and the selfish. Be merciful, even as your Father is merciful."

TWENTIETH SUNDAY

Verse: Sing praises to our God, sing praises.
Clap your hands, all you nations.
The reading is from Paul's Letter to the Galatians.
Chapter 1.11-19.

Brethren, I would have you know that the gospel which was preached by me is not man's gospel. For I did not receive it from man, nor was I taught it, but it came through a revelation of Jesus Christ. For you have heard of my former life in Judaism, how I persecuted the church of God violently and tried to destroy it; and I advanced in Judaism beyond many of my own age among my people, so extremely jealous was I for the traditions of my fathers. But when he who had set me apart before I was born, and had called me through his grace, was pleased to reveal his Son to me, in order that I might preach him among the Gentiles, I did not confer with flesh and blood, nor did I go up to Jerusalem to those who were apostles before me, but I went away into Arabia; and again I returned to Damascus. Then, after three years I went up to Jerusalem to visit Cephas, and remained with him fifteen days. But I saw none of the other apostles except James, the Lord's brother.

THE GOSPEL READING
Luke 7.11-16.

At that time Jesus went to a city called Nain, and his disciples and a great crowd went with him. As he drew near to the gate of the city, behold, a man who had died was being carried out, the only son of his mother, and a large crowd from the city was with her. And when the Lord saw her, he had compassion on her and said to her, "Do not weep." And he came and touched the bier, and the bearers stood still. And he said, "Young man, I say to you, arise." And the dead man sat up, and began to speak. And he gave him to his mother. Fear seized them all; and they glorified God, saying, "A great prophet has arisen among us!" and "God has visited his people!"

TWENTY-FIRST SUNDAY

Verse: O Lord, how magnificent are your works.
    You have made all things in wisdom.
    Bless the Lord, O my soul.
The reading is from Paul's Letter to the Galatians.
Chapter 2.16-20.

Brethren, you know that a man is not justified by works of the law but through faith in Jesus Christ, even we have believed in Christ Jesus, in order to be justified by faith in Christ, and not by works of the law, because by works of the law shall no one be justified. But if, in our endeavor to be justified in Christ, we ourselves were found to be sinners, is Christ then an agent of sin? Certainly not! But if I build up again those things which I tore down, then I prove myself a transgressor. For I, through the law, died to the law, that I might live to God. I have been crucified with Christ; it is no longer I who live, but Christ who lives in me; and the life I now live in the flesh I live by faith in the Son of God, who loved me and gave himself for me.

98

THE GOSPEL READING
Luke 8.5-15.

The Lord said this parable: "A sower went out to sow his seed; and as he sowed, some fell along the path, and was trodden under foot, and the birds of the air devoured it. And some fell on the rock; and as it grew up, it withered away, because it had no moisture. And some fell among thorns; and the thorns grew with it and choked it. And some fell into good soil and grew, and yielded a hundredfold."

And when his disciples asked him what this parable meant, he said, "To you it has been given to know the secrets of the kingdom of God; but for others they are in parables, so that seeing they may not see, and hearing they may not understand. Now the parable is this: The seed is the word of God. The ones along the path are those who have heard; then the devil comes and takes away the word from their hearts, that they may not believe and be saved. And the ones on the rock are those who, when they hear the word, receive it with joy; but these have no root, they believe for a while and in time of temptation fall away. And as for what fell among the thorns, they are those who hear, but as they go on their way they are choked by the cares and riches and pleasures of life, and their fruit does not mature. And as for that in the good soil, they are those who, hearing the word, hold it fast in an honest and good heart, and bring forth fruit with patience." As he said these things, he cried out "He who has ears to hear, let him hear."

TWENTY-SECOND SUNDAY

Verse: You, O Lord, shall keep us and preserve us.
Save me, O Lord,
for the godly man has failed.

The reading is from Paul's Letter to the Galatians.
Chapter 6.11-18.

Brethren, see with what large letters I am writing to you with my own hand. It is those who want to make a good showing in the flesh that would compel you to be circumcised, and only in order that they may not be persecuted for the cross of Christ. For even those who receive circumcision do not themselves keep the law, but they desire to have you circumcised that they may glory in your flesh. But far be it from me to glory except in the cross of our Lord Jesus Christ, by which the world has been crucified to me, and I to the world. For neither circumcision counts for anything, nor uncircumcision, but a new creation. Peace and mercy be upon all who walk by this rule, upon the Israel of God.

Henceforth, let no man trouble me; for I bear on my body the marks of Jesus.

The grace of our Lord Jesus Christ be with your spirit, brethren. Amen.

THE GOSPEL READING
Luke 16.19-31.

The Lord said: ''There was a rich man, who was clothed in purple and fine linen and who feasted sumptuously every day. And at his gate lay a poor man named Lazaros, full of sores, who desired to be fed with what fell from the rich man's table; moreover the dogs came and licked his sores. The poor man died and was carried by the angels to Abraham's bosom. The rich man also died and was buried; and in Hades, being in torment, he lifted up his eyes, and saw Abraham far off and Lazaros in his bosom. And he called out, 'Father Abraham, have mercy upon me, and send Lazaros to dip the end of his finger in water and cool my tongue; for I am in anguish in this flame.' But Abraham said, 'Son, remember that you in your lifetime received your good things, and Lazaros in like manner evil things; but now he is comforted here, and you are in anguish. And besides all this, between us and you a great chasm has been fixed, in order that those who would pass from here to you may not be able, and none may cross from there to us.' And he said, 'Then I beg you, father, to send him to my father's house, for I have five brothers, so that he may warn them, lest they also come into this place of torment.' But Abraham said, 'They have Moses, and the prophets; let them hear them.' And he said, 'No, father Abraham; but if some one goes to them from the dead, they will repent.' He said to them, 'If they do not hear Moses and the prophets, neither will they be convinced if some one should rise from the dead.' "

TWENTY-THIRD SUNDAY

Verse: O Lord, save your people
and bless your inheritance.

To you, O Lord, have I cried, O my God.
The reading is from Paul's Letter to the Ephesians.
Chapter 2.4-10.

Brethren, God, who is rich in mercy, out of the great love with which he loved us, even when we were dead through our trespasses, made us alive together with Christ (by grace you have been saved), and raised us up with him in the heavenly places in Christ Jesus, that in the coming ages he might show the immeasurable riches of his grace in kindness toward us in Christ Jesus. For by grace you have been saved through faith; and this is not your own doing, it is the gift of God— not because of works, lest any man should boast. For we are his workmanship, created in Christ Jesus for good works, which God prepared beforehand, that we should walk in them.

THE GOSPEL READING
Luke 8.26-39.

At that time, as Jesus arrived at the country of the Gerasenes, there met him a man from the city who had demons; for a long time he had worn no clothes and he lived not in a house but among the tombs. When he saw Jesus, he cried out and fell down before him, and said with a loud voice, ''What have you to do with me, Jesus, Son of the Most High God? I beseech you, do not torment me.''

For he had commanded the unclean spirit to come out of the man. (For many a time it had seized him; he was kept under guard, and bound with chains and fetters, but he broke the bonds and was driven by the

102

demon into the desert.) Jesus then asked him, "What is your name?" And he said, "Legion"; for many demons had entered him. And they begged him not to command them to depart into the abyss. Now a large herd of swine was feeding there on the hillside; and they begged him to let them enter these. So he gave them leave. Then the demons came out of the man and entered the swine, and the herd rushed down the steep bank into the lake and were drowned.

When the herdsmen saw what happened, they fled, and told it in the city and in the country. Then people went out to see what had happened, and they came to Jesus, and found the man from whom the demons had gone, sitting at the feet of Jesus, clothed and in his right mind; and they were afraid. And those who had seen it told them how he who had been possessed with demons was healed. Then all the people of the surrounding country of the Gerasenes asked him to depart from them; for they were seized with great fear; so he got into the boat and returned. The man from whom the demons had gone begged that he might be with him; but he sent him away, saying, "Return to your home, and declare how much God has done for you." And he went away, proclaiming throughout the whole city how much Jesus had done for him.

TWENTY-FOURTH SUNDAY

Verse: The Lord will give strength to his people.
Bring to the Lord, O Sons of God,
bring to the Lord honor and glory.

The reading is from Paul's Letter to the Ephesians.
Chapter 2.14-22.

Brethren, he is our peace, who has made us both one, and has broken down the dividing wall of hostility, by abolishing in his flesh the law of commandments and ordinances, that he might create in himself one new man in place of the two, so making peace, and might reconcile us both to God in one body through the cross, thereby bringing the hostility to an end. And he came and preached peace to you who were far off and peace to those who were near; for through him we both have access in one Spirit to the Father. So then you are no longer strangers and sojourners, but you are fellow citizens with saints and members of the household of God, built upon the foundation of the apostles and prophets, Christ Jesus himself being cornerstone, in whom the whole structure is joined together and grows into a holy temple in the Lord; in whom you also are built into it for a dwelling place of God in the Spirit.

THE GOSPEL READING
Luke 8.41-56.

At that time, there came to Jesus a man named Jairus, who was a ruler of the synagogue; and falling at Jesus' feet he besought him to come to his house, for he had an only daughter, about twelve years of age, and she was dying.

As he went, the people pressed round him. And a woman who had had a flow of blood for twelve years and had spent all her living upon physicians and could not be healed by anyone, came up behind him, and touched the fringe of his garment; and immediately her flow of blood ceased. And Jesus said, "Who was it that touched me?" When all denied it, Peter said, "Master, the multitudes surround you and press upon you!" But Jesus said, "Some one touched me; for I perceive that power has gone forth from me." And when the woman saw that she was not hidden, she came trembling, and falling down before him declared in the presence of all the people why she had touched him, and how she had been immediately healed. And he said to her, "Daughter, your faith has made you well; go in peace."

While he was still speaking, a man from the ruler's house came and said, "Your daughter is dead; do not trouble the Teacher any more." But Jesus on hearing this answered him, "Do not fear; only believe, and she shall be well." And when he came to the house, he permitted no one to enter with him, except Peter and John and James, and the father and mother of the child. And all were weeping and bewailing her; but he said, "Do not weep; for she is not dead but sleeping." And they laughed at him, knowing that she was dead. But taking her by the hand he called, saying, "Child, arise." And her spirit returned, and she got up at once; and he directed that something should be given her to eat. And her parents were amazed; but he charged them to tell no one what had happened.

TWENTY-FIFTH SUNDAY

Verse: Make your vows to the Lord
our God and perform them.
God is known in Judah; his name
is great in Israel.

The reading is from Paul's Letter to the Ephesians.
Chapter 4.1-7.

Brethren, I, therefore, a prisoner for the Lord, beg you to lead a life worthy of the calling to which you have been called, with all lowliness and meekness, with patience, forbearing with one another in love, eager to maintain the unity of the spirit in the bond of peace. There is one body and one spirit, just as you were called to the one hope that belongs to your call, one Lord, one faith, one baptism, one God and Father of us all, who is above all and through all and in all. But grace was given to each of us according to the measure of Christ's gift.

THE GOSPEL READING
Luke 10.25-37.

At that time, a lawyer stood up to put Jesus to the test, saying, "Teacher, what shall I do to inherit eternal life?" He said to him, "What is written in the law? How do you read?" And he answered, "You shall love the Lord your God with all your heart, and with all your soul, and with all your strength, and with all your mind; and your neighbor as yourself." And he said to him, "You have answered right; do this, and you will live."

But he, desiring to justify himself, said to Jesus, "And who is my neighbor?" Jesus replied, "A man was going down from Jerusalem to Jericho, and he fell among robbers, who stripped him and beat him, and departed, leaving him half dead. Now by chance a priest was going down that road; and when he saw him he passed by on the other side. So likewise a Levite, when he came to the place and saw him, passed by on the other side. But a Samaritan, as he journeyed, came to where he was; and when he saw him, he had compassion, and went to him and bound up his wounds, pouring on oil and wine; then he set him on his own beast and brought him to an inn, and took care of him. And the next day he took out two denarii and gave them to the innkeeper, saying, 'Take care of him; and whatever more you spend, I will repay you when I come back.' Which of these three, do you think, proved neighbor to the man who fell among the robbers?" He said, "The one who showed mercy on him." And Jesus said to him, "Go and do likewise."

TWENTY-SIXTH SUNDAY

Verse: Let your mercy, O Lord, be upon us.
Rejoice in the Lord, O you righteous.
The reading is from Paul's Letter to the Ephesians.
Chapter 5.8-19.
Brethren, walk as children of light (for the fruit of light is found in all that is good and right and true), and try to learn what is pleasing to the Lord. Take no part in the unfruitful works of darkness, but instead

expose them. For it is a shame even to speak of the things that they do in secret; but when anything is exposed by the light it becomes visible, for anything that becomes visible is light. Therefore it is said,

"Awake, O sleeper, and arise from the dead, and Christ shall give you light."

Look carefully then how you walk, not as unwise men but as wise, making the most of the time, because the days are evil. Therefore do not be foolish, but understand what the will of the Lord is. And do not get drunk with wine, for that is debauchery; but be filled with the Spirit, addressing one another in psalms and hymns and spiritual songs, singing and making melody to the Lord with all your heart, always and for everything giving thanks in the name of our Lord Jesus Christ to God the Father.

THE GOSPEL READING
Luke 12.16-21.

The Lord said this parable: "The land of a rich man brought forth plentifully; and he thought to himself, 'What shall I do, for I have nowhere to store my crops?' And he said, 'I will do this: I will pull down my barns, and build larger ones; and there I will store all my grain and my goods. And I will say to my soul, 'Soul, you have ample goods laid up for many years; take your ease, eat, drink, be merry.' But God said to him, 'Fool! This night your soul is required of you; and the things you have prepared, whose will they be?' So is he who lays up treasure for himself, and is not rich toward God." As he said these things, he cried out: "He who has ears to hear, let him hear."

TWENTY-SEVENTH SUNDAY

Verse: The Lord is my strength and my song.
The Lord has chastened me sorely.
The reading is from Paul's Letter to the Ephesians.
Chapter 6.10-17.

Brethren, be strong in the Lord and in the strength of his might. Put on the whole armor of God, that you may be able to stand against the wiles of the devil. For we are not contending against flesh and blood, but against the principalities, against the powers, against the world rulers of this present darkness, against the spiritual hosts of wickedness in the heavenly places. Therefore take the whole armor of God, that you may be able to withstand in the evil day, and having done all, to stand. Stand therefore, having girded your loins with truth, and having put on the breastplate of righteousness, and having shod your feet with the equipment of the gospel of peace; besides all these, taking the shield of faith, with which you can quench all the flaming darts of the evil one. And take the helmet of salvation, and the sword of the Spirit, which is the word of God.

THE GOSPEL READING
Luke 13.10-17.

At that time, Jesus was teaching in one of the

synagogues on the sabbath. And there was a woman who had a spirit of infirmity for eighteen years; she was bent over and could not fully straighten herself. And when Jesus saw her, he called her and said to her, "Woman, you are freed from your infirmity." And he laid his hands upon her, and immediately she was made straight, and she praised God. But the ruler of the synagogue, indignant because Jesus had healed on the sabbath, said to the people, "There are six days on which work ought to be done; come on those days and be healed, and not on the sabbath day." Then the Lord answered him, "You hypocrites! Does not each of you on the sabbath untie his ox or his ass from the manger, and lead it away to water it? And ought not this woman, a daughter of Abraham whom Satan bound for eighteen years, be loosed from this bond on the sabbath day?" As he said this, all his adversaries were put to shame; and all the people rejoiced at all the glorious things that were done by him.

TWENTY-EIGHTH SUNDAY

Verse: Sing praises to our God, sing praises.
Clap your hands, all you nations.
The reading is from Paul's Letter to the Colossians.
Chapter 1.12-18.
Brethren, we give thanks to the Father, who has qualified us to share in the inheritance of the saints in light. He has delivered us from the dominion of darkness and transferred us to the kingdom of his beloved Son, in whom we have redemption, the

forgiveness of sins.

He is the image of the invisible God, the first-born of all creation; for in him all things were created, in heaven and on earth, visible and invisible, whether thrones or dominions or principalities or authorities— all things were created through him and for him. He is before all things, and in him all things hold together. He is the head of the body, the church; he is the beginning, the first-born from the dead, that in everything he might be preeminent.

THE GOSPEL READING
Luke 14.16-24.

The Lord said this parable: "A man once gave a great banquet, and invited many; and at the time of the banquet he sent his servant to say to those who had been invited, 'Come; for all is now ready.' But they all alike began to make excuses. The first said to him, 'I have bought a field, and I go out and see it; I pray you, have me excused.' And another said, 'I have bought five yoke of oxen, and I must go to examine them; I pray you, have me excused.' And another said, 'I have married a wife, and therefore I cannot come.' So the servant came and reported this to his master. Then the householder in anger said to his servant, 'Go out quickly to the streets and lanes of the city, and bring in the poor and maimed and blind and lame.' And the servant said, 'Sir, what you commanded has been done, and there is still room.' And the master said to the servant, 'Go out to the highways and hedges, and compel people to come in,

111

that my house may be filled. For I tell you, none of those men who were invited shall taste my banquet. For many are called, but few are chosen.' "

TWENTY-NINTH SUNDAY

Verse: O Lord, how magnificent are your works.
You have made all things in wisdom.
Bless the Lord, O my soul.
The reading is from Paul's Letter to the Colossians.
Chapter 3.4-11.

Brethren, when Christ who is our life appears, then you also will appear with him in glory.

Put to death therefore what is earthly in you; fornication, impurity, passion, evil desire, and covetousness, which is idolatry. On account of these the wrath of God is coming upon the sins of disobedience. In these you once walked, when you lived in them. But now put them all away: anger, wrath, malice, slander, and foul talk from your mouth. Do not lie to one another, seeing that you have put off the old nature with its practices and have put on the new nature, which is being renewed in knowledge after the image of its creator. Here there cannot be Greek and Jew, circumcised and uncircumcised, barbarian, Scythian, slave, free man, but Christ is all, and in all.

THE GOSPEL READING
Luke 17.12-19.

At that time, as Jesus entered a village, he was met by ten lepers, who stood at a distance and lifted up

112

their voices and said, "Jesus, Master, have mercy on us." When he saw them he said to them, "Go and show yourselves to the priests." And as they went they were cleansed. Then one of them, when he saw that he was healed, turned back, praising God with a loud voice; and he fell on his face at Jesus' feet, giving him thanks. Now he was a Samaritan. Then said Jesus, "Were not ten cleansed? Where are the nine? Was no one found to return and give praise to God except this foreigner?" And he said to him, "Rise and go your way; your faith has made you well."

THIRTIETH SUNDAY

Verse: You, O Lord, shall keep us and preserve us.
Save me, O Lord, for the godly man has failed.
The reading is from Paul's Letter to the Colossians.
Chapter 8.12-16.
Brethren, put on as God's chosen ones, holy and beloved, compassion, kindness, lowliness, meekness, and patience, forbearing with one another and, if one has a complaint against another, forgiving each other; as the Lord has forgiven you, so you also must forgive. And above all these put on love, which binds everything together in perfect harmony. And let the peace of Christ rule in your hearts, to which indeed you were called in the one body. And be thankful. Let the word of Christ dwell in you richly, teach and admonish one another in all wisdom, and sing psalms and hymns and spiritual songs with thankfulness in your hearts to God.

113

THE GOSPEL READING
Luke 18.18-27.

At that time, a ruler came to Jesus and asked him, "Good Teacher, what shall I do to inherit eternal life?" And Jesus said to him, "Why do you call me good? No one is good but God alone. You know the commandments: 'Do not commit adultery, Do not kill, Do not steal, Do not bear false witness, Honor your father and mother.' " And he said, "All these I have observed from my youth." And when Jesus heard it, he said to him, "One things you still lack. Sell all that you have and distribute it to the poor, and you will have treasure in heaven; and come, follow me." But when he heard this he became sad, for he was very rich. Jesus looking at him said, "How hard it is for those who have riches to enter the kingdom of God! For it is easier for a camel to go through the eye of a needle than for a rich man to enter the kingdom of God." Those who heard it said, "Then who can be saved?" But he said, "What is impossible with men is possible with God."

THIRTY-FIRST SUNDAY

Verse: O Lord, save your people,
and bless your inheritance.
To you, O Lord, have I cried, O my God.
The reading is from Paul's First Letter to Timothy.
Chapter 1.15-17.

Timothy, my son, the saying is sure and worthy of full acceptance, that Christ Jesus came into the world to save sinners. And I am the foremost of sinners; but I received mercy for this reason, that in me, as the foremost, Jesus Christ might display his perfect patience for an example to those who were to believe in him for eternal life. To the King of ages, immortal, invisible, the only God, be honor and glory forever and ever. Amen.

THE GOSPEL READING
Luke 18.35-43.

At that time, as Jesus drew near to Jericho, a blind man was sitting by the roadside begging; and hearing a multitude going by, he inquired what this meant. They told him, "Jesus of Nazareth is passing by." And he cried, "Jesus, Son of David, have mercy on me!" And those who were in front rebuked him, telling him to be silent; but he cried out all the more, "Son of David, have mercy on me!" And Jesus stopped, and commanded him to be brought to him; and when he came near, he asked him, "What do you want me to do for you?" He said, "Lord, let me receive my sight." And Jesus said to him, "Receive your sight; your faith has made you well." And immediately he received his sight and followed him, glorifying God; and all the people, when they saw it, gave praise to God.

THIRTY-SECOND SUNDAY

Verse: The Lord will give strength to his people.

Bring to the Lord, O sons of God,
bring to the Lord honor and glory.
The reading is from Paul's First Letter to Timothy.
Chapter 4.9-15.

Timothy, my son, the saying is sure and worthy of full acceptance. For to this end we toil and strive, because we have our hope set on the living God, who is the Savior of all men, especially of those who believe.

Command and teach these things. Let no one despise your youth, but set the believers an example in speech and conduct, in love, in faith, in purity. Till I come, attend to the public reading of scripture, to preaching, to teaching. Do not neglect the gift you have, which was given you by prophetic utterance when the elders laid their hands upon you. Practice these duties, devote yourself to them, so that all may see your progress.

THE GOSPEL READING
Luke 19.1-10.

At that time, Jesus entered Jericho and was passing through. And there was a man named Zacchaios; he was a chief tax collector, and rich. And he sought to see who Jesus was, but could not, on account of the crowd, because he was small of stature. So he ran on ahead and climbed up into a sycamore tree to see him, for he was to pass that way. And when Jesus came to the place, he looked up and said to him, ''Zacchaios, make haste and come down; for I must stay at your house today.'' So he made haste and came

116

down,and received him joyfully. And when they saw it they all murmured, "He has gone in to be the guest of a man who is a sinner." And Zacchaios stood and said to the Lord, "Behold, Lord, the half of my goods I give to the poor; and if I have defrauded any one of anything, I restore it fourfold." And Jesus said to him, "Today salvation has come to this house, since he also is a son of Abraham. For the Son of man came to seek and to save the lost."

SUNDAY OF THE FOREFATHERS

Verse: Blessed are you, O Lord,
 the God of our Fathers.
For you are just in all you have done.
The reading is from Paul's Letter to the Colossians.
Chapter 3.4-11.

Brethren, when Christ who is our life appears, then you also will appear with him in glory. Put to death therefore what is earthly in you: immorality, impurity, passion, evil desire, and covetousness, which is idolatry. On account of these the wrath of God is coming. In these you once walked when you lived in them. But now put them all away: anger, wrath, malice, slander, and foul talk from your mouth. Do not lie to one another, seeing that you have put off the old nature with its practices and have put on the new nature, which is being renewed in knowledge after the image of its creator. Here there cannot be Greek and Jew, circumcised, uncircumcised, barbarian, Scythian, slave, free man, but Christ is all, and in all.

THE GOSPEL READING
Luke 14.16-24.

The Lord said: "A man once gave a great banquet, and invited many; and at the time of the banquet he sent his servants to say to those who had been invited, 'Come; for all is now ready.' But they all alike began to make excuses. The first said to him, 'I have bought a field, and I must go out and see it; I pray you, have me excused.' And another said, 'I have bought five yoke of oxen and I go to examine them; I pray you have me excused.' And another said, 'I have married a wife, and therefore I cannot come.' So the servant came and reported this to his master. Then the householder in anger said to his servant, 'Go out quickly to the streets and lanes of the city, and bring in the poor and maimed and blind and lame.' And the servant said, 'Sir, what you commanded has been done, and still there is room.' And the master said to the servant, 'Go out to the highways and hedges, and compel people to come in, that my house may be filled. For I tell you, none of those men who were invited shall taste my banquet. For many are called, but few are chosen.' "

SUNDAY BEFORE CHRISTMAS

Verse: Blessed are you, O Lord,
the God of our Father
For you are just in all you have done.
The reading is from Paul's Letter to the Hebrews.
Chapter 11.9-10, 32-40.
Brethren, by faith Abraham sojourned in the land of promise, as in a foreign land, living in tents with Isaac

and Jacob, heirs with him of the same promise. For he looked forward to the city which has foundations, whose builder and maker is God. And what more shall I say? For time will fail me to tell of Gideon, Barak, Samson, Jephthah, of David and Samuel and the prophets—who through faith conquered kingdoms, and enforced justice, received promises, stopped the mouths of lions, quenched raging fire, escaped the edge of the sword, won strength out of weakness, became mighty in war, put foreign armies to flight. Women received their dead by resurrection. Some were tortured, refusing to accept relese, that they might rise again to a better life. Others suffered mocking and scourging, and even chains and imprisonment. They were stoned, they were sawn in two, they were killed with the sword; they went about in skins of sheep and goats, destitute, afflicted, ill-treated (of whom the world is not worthy) wandering over deserts and mountains, and in dens and caves of the earth. And all these, though well attested by their faith, did not receive what was promised, since God had foreseen something better for us, that apart from us they should not be made perfect.

THE GOSPEL READING
Matthew 1.1-25.

The book of the genealogy of Jesus Christ, the son of David, the son of Abraham.

Abraham was the father of Isaac, and Isaac the father of Jacob, and Jacob the father of Judah and his brothers, and Judah the father of Perez and Zerah by Tamar, and Perez the father of Hezron, and

119

Hezron the father of Ram, and Ram the father of Amminadab, and Amminadab the father of Nashon, and Nahshon the father of Salmon, and Salmon the father of Boaz by Rahab, and Boaz the father of Obed by Ruth, and Obed the father of Jesse, and Jesse the father of David the king.

And David was the father of Solomon by the wife of Uriah, and Solomon the father of Rehoboam, and Rehoboam the father of Abijah, and Abijah the father of Asa, and Asa the father of Jehoshaphat, and Jehoshaphat the father of Joram, and Joram the father of Uzziah, and Uzziah the father of Jotham, and Jotham the father of Ahaz, and Ahaz the father of Hezekiah, and Hezekiah the father of Manasseh, and Manasseh the father of Amos, and Amos the father of Josiah, and Josiah the father of Jechoniah and his brothers, at the time of the deportation to Babylon.

And after the deportation to Babylon: Jechoniah was the father of Shealtiel, and Shealtiel the father of Zerubbabel, and Zerubbabel the father of Abiud, and Abiud the father of Eliakim, and Eliakim the father of Azor, and Azor the father of Zadok, and Zadok the father of Achim, and Achim the father of Eliud, and Eliud the father of Eleazar, and Eleazar the father of Matthan, and Matthan the father of Jacob, and Jacob the father of Joseph, the husband of Mary, of whom Jesus was born, who is called Christ.

So all the generations from Abraham to David were fourteen generations, and from David to the deportation to Babylon fourteen generations, and from the deportation to Babylon to the Christ fourteen generations.

120

Now the birth of Jesus Christ took place in this way. When his mother Mary had been betrothed to Joseph, before they came together she was found to be with child of the Holy Spirit; and her husband Joseph, being a just man and unwilling to put her to shame, resolved to send her away quietly. But as he considered this, behold, an angel of the Lord appeared to him in a dream, saying, "Joseph, son of David, do not fear to take Mary your wife, for that which is conceived in her is of the Holy Spirit; she will bear a son, and you shall call his name Jesus, for he will save his people from their sins." All this took place to fulfill what the Lord had spoken by the prophet:

"Behold, a virgin shall conceive and bear a son,
   and his name shall be called Emmanuel"
(which means, God with us). When Joseph woke from sleep, he did as the angel of the Lord commanded him; he took his wife, but knew her not until she had borne a son; and he called his name Jesus.

CHRISTMAS DAY

Verse: Let all the earth worship you,
   and sing to you.
Shout with joy to God, all the earth.
The reading is from Paul's Letter to the Galatians.
Chapter 4.4-7.
Brethren, when the time had fully come, God sent forth his Son, born of woman, born under the law, to redeem those who were under the law, so that we might receive adoption as sons. And because you are sons, God has sent the Spirit of his Son into our hearts,

crying, "Abba! Father!" So through God you are no longer a slave but a son, and if a son then an heir.

THE GOSPEL READING
Matthew 2.1-12.

When Jesus was born in Bethlehem of Judea in the days of Herod the king, behold, wise men from the East came to Jerusalem, saying, "Where is he who has been born king of the Jews? For we have seen his star in the East, and have come to worship him." When Herod the king heard this, he was troubled, and all Jerusalem with him; and assembling all the chief priests and scribes of the people, he inquired of them where the Christ was to be born. They told him, "In Bethlehem of Judea; for so it is written by the prophet:

'And you, O Bethlehem, in the land of Judah,
are by no means least among the rulers of Judah;
for from you shall come a ruler
who will govern my people Israel.' "

Then Herod summoned the wise men secretly and ascertained from them what time the star appeared; and he sent them to Bethlehem, saying, "Go and search diligently for the child, and when you have found him bring me word, that I too may come and worship him." When they had heard the king they went their way; and lo, the star which they had seen in the East went before them, till it came to rest over the place where the child was. When they saw the star, they rejoiced exceedingly with great joy; and going into the house they saw the child with Mary his mother, and they fell down and worshiped him. Then, open-

122

ing their treasures, they offered him gifts, gold and
frankincense and myrrh. And being warned in a dream
not to return to Herod, they departed to their own
country by another way.

SUNDAY AFTER CHRISTMAS

Verse: God is wonderful among the saints.
Bless God in the congregations.
The reading is from Paul's Letter to the Galatians.
Chapter 1.11-19.

Brethren, I would have you know, that the gospel
which was preached by me is not man's gospel. For
I did not receive it from man, nor was I taught it, but
it came through a revelation of Jesus Christ. For you
have heard of my former life in Judaism, how I
persecuted the church of God violently and tried to
destroy it; and I advanced in Judaism beyond many
of my own age among my people, so extremely zealous
was I for the traditions of my fathers. But when he
who had set me apart before I was born, and had called
me through his grace, was pleased to reveal his Son
to me, in order that I might preach him among the
Gentiles, I did not confer with flesh and blood, nor
did I go up to Jerusalem to those who were apostles
before me, but I went away into Arabia; and again
I returned to Damascus.

Then after three years I went up to Jerusalem to visit
Cephas, and remained with him fifteen days. But I saw
none of the other apostles except James the Lord's
brother.

123

THE GOSPEL READING
Matthew 2.13-23.

When the Magi had departed, behold, an angel of the Lord appeared to Joseph in a dream and said, "Rise, take the child and his mother, and flee to Egypt, and remain there till I tell you; for Herod is about to search for the child, to destroy him." And he rose and took the child and his mother by night, and departed to Egypt, and remained there until the death of Herod. This was to fulfill what the Lord has spoken by the prophet, "Out of Egypt have I called my son."

Then Herod, when he saw that he had been tricked by the wise men, was in a furious rage, and he sent and killed all the male children in Bethlehem and in all that region who were two years old or under, according to the time which he had ascertained from the wise men. Then was fulfilled what was spoken by the prophet Jeremiah:

"A voice was heard in Ramah,
wailing and loud lamentation,
Rachel weeping for her children;
she refused to be consoled,
because they were no more."

But when Herod died, behold, an angel of the Lord appeared in a dream to Joseph in Egypt, saying, "Rise, take the child and his mother, and go to the land of Israel, for those who sought the child's life are dead." And he rose and took the child and his mother, and went to the land of Israel. But when he heard that Archelaos reigned over Judea in place of his father Herod, he was afraid to go there, and being warned in a dream he withdrew to the district of Galilee. And he went and dwelt in a city called Nazareth that what was spoken by the prophets might be fulfilled, "He shall be called a Nazarene."

SUNDAY BEFORE THEOPHANY

Verse: O Lord, save your people and bless
your inheritance.
To you, O Lord, have I cried, O my God.
The reading is from Paul's Second Letter to Timothy.
Chapter 4.5-8.

Timothy, my son, always be steady, endure suffering, do the work of an evangelist, fulfill your ministry.

For I am already on the point of being sacrificed; the time of my departure has come. I have fought the good fight, I have finished the race, I have kept the faith. Henceforth there is laid up for me the crown of righteousness, which the Lord, the righteous judge, will award to me on that Day, and not only to me but also to all who have loved his appearing.

THE GOSPEL READING
Mark 1.1-8.

The beginning of the gospel of Jesus Christ, the Son of God.

As it is written in Isaiah the prophet,
"Behold, I send my messenger before thy face,
who shall prepare thy way;
the voice of one crying in the wilderness:
Prepare the way of the Lord,
make his paths straight—"
John the baptizer appeared in the wilderness, preaching a baptism of repentance for the forgiveness of sins. And there went out to him all the country of Judea, and all the people of Jerusalem; and they were

baptized by him in the river Jordan, confessing their sins. Now John was clothed with camel's hair, and had a leather girdle around his waist, and ate locusts and wild honey. And he preached, saying, "After me comes he who is mightier than I, the one whose sandals I am not worthy to stoop down and untie. I have baptized you with water; but he will baptize you with the Holy Spirit."

DAY OF THEOPHANY

Verse: Blessed is he who comes in the name
of the Lord.
Give thanks to the Lord, for he is good.
The reading is from Paul's Letter to Titus.
Chapters 2.11-14;3.4-7.

Titus, my son, the grace of God has appeared for the salvation of all men, training us to renounce irreligion and worldly passions, and to live sober, upright, and godly lives in this world, awaiting our blessed hope, the appearing of the glory of our God and Savior Jesus Christ, who gave himself for us to redeem us from all iniquity and to purity for himself a people of his own who are zealous for good deeds; when the goodness and loving kindness of God our Savior appeared, he saved us, not because of deeds done by us in righteousness, but in virtue of his own mercy, by the washing of regeneration and renewal in the Holy Spirit, which he poured out upon us richly through Jesus Christ our Savior, so that we might be justified by his grace and become heirs in hope of eternal life.

THE GOSPEL READING
Mark 3.13-17.

Then Jesus came from Galilee to the Jordan to John, to be baptized by him. John would have prevented him, saying, "I need to be baptized by you, and do you come to me?" But Jesus answered him, "Let it be so now; for thus it is fitting for us to fulfill all righteousness." Then he consented. And when Jesus was baptized, he went up immediately from the water, and behold, the heavens were opened and he saw the Spirit of God descending like a dove, and alighting on him; and lo, a voice from heaven, saying, "This is my beloved Son, with whom I am well pleased."

SUNDAY AFTER THEOPHANY

Verse: Let your mercy, O Lord, be upon us.
Rejoice in the Lord, O you righteous.
The reading is from Paul's Letter to the Ephesians.
Chapter 4.7-13.

Brethren, grace was given to each of us according to the measure of Christ's gift. Therefore it is said,

"When he ascended on high he led a host of captives, and he gave gifts to men."

(In saying, "He ascended," what does it mean but that he had also descended into the lower parts of the earth? He who descended is he who also ascended far above all the heavens, that he might fill all things.) And his gifts were that some should be apostles, some prophets, some evangelists, some pastors and teachers,

127

to equip the saints for the work of ministry, for building up the body of Christ, until we all attain to the unity of the faith and of the knowledge of the Son of God, to mature manhood, to the measure of the stature of the fulness of Christ.

THE GOSPEL READING
Matthew 4.12-17.

At that time, when Jesus heard that John had been arrested, he withdrew into Galilee; and leaving Nazareth he went and dwelt in Capernaum by the sea, in the territory of Zebulum and the land of Naphtali, that what was spoken by the prophet Isaiah might be fulfilled:

"The land of Zebulum and the land of Naphtali,
toward the sea, across the Jordan,
Galilee of the Gentiles—
the people who sat in darkness
have seen a great light,
and for those who sat in the region
and shadow of death light has dawned."

From that time Jesus began to preach, saying, "Repent, for the kingdom of heaven is at hand."

SUNDAY OF THE PUBLICAN AND PHARISEE

Verse: Make your vows to the Lord our God
and perform them.
God is known in Judah;
his name is great in Israel.

128

The reading is from Paul's Second Letter to Timothy.
Chapter 3.10-15.

Timothy, my son, you have observed my teaching, my conduct, my aim in life, my faith, my patience, my love, my steadfastness, my persecutions, my sufferings, what befell me at Antioch, at Iconion, and at Lystra, what persecutions I endured; yet from them all the Lord rescued me. Indeed all who desire to live a godly life in Christ Jesus will be persecuted, while evil men and impostors will go on from bad to worse, deceivers and deceived. But as for you, continue in what you have learned and have firmly believed, knowing from whom you learned it and how from childhood you have been acquainted with the sacred writings which are able to instruct you for salvation through faith in Christ Jesus.

THE GOSPEL READING
Luke 18.10-14.

The Lord said this parable: "Two men went up into the temple to pray, one a Pharisee and the other a tax collector. The Pharisee stood and prayed thus with himself, 'God, I thank Thee that I am not like other men, extortioners, unjust, adulterers, or even like this tax collector. I fast twice a week, I give tithes of all that I get.' But the tax collector, standing far off, would not even lift up his eyes to heaven, but beat his breast, saying, 'God, be merciful to me a sinner!' I tell you, this man went down to his house justified rather than the other; for everyone who exalts himself will be humbled, but he who humbles himself will be exalted."

SUNDAY OF THE PRODIGAL SON

Verse: Let your mercy, O Lord, be upon us.
Rejoice in the Lord, O you righteous.
The reading is from Paul's First Letter to the
Corinthians.
Chapter 6.12-20.

Brethren, "All things are lawful for me," but not all
things are helpful. "All things are lawful for me," but
I will not be enslaved by anything. "Food is meant
for the stomach and the stomach for food"—and God
will destroy both one and the other. The body is not
meant for immorality, but for the Lord, and the Lord
for the body. And God raised the Lord and will also
raise us up by his power. Do you not know that your
bodies are members of Christ? Shall I therefore take
the members of Christ and make them members of a
prostitute? Never! Do you not know that he who joins
himself to a prostitute become one body with her? For,
as it is written, "The two shall become one flesh." But
he who is united to the Lord becomes one spirit with
him. Shun immorality. Every other sin which a man
commmits is outside the body. Do you not know that
your body is a temple of the Holy Spirit within you,
which you have from God? You are not your own;
you were bought with a price. So glorify God in your
body.

THE GOSPEL READING
Luke 15.11-32.
The Lord said this parable: "There was a man who

had two sons; and the younger of them said to his father, 'Father, give me the share of the property that falls to me.' And he divided his living between them. Not many days later, the younger son gathered all he had and took his journey into a far country, and there he squandered his property in loose living. And when he had spent everything, a great famine arose in that country, and he began to be in want. So he went and joined himself to one of the citizens of that country, who sent him into his fields to feed swine. And he would gladly have fed on the pods that the swine ate; and no one gave him anything. But when he came to himself he said, 'How many of my father's hired servants have bread enough and to spare, but I perish here with hunger! I will arise and go to my father, and I will say to him, "Father, I have sinned against heaven and before you; I am no longer worthy to be called your son; treat me as one of your hired servants." ' And he arose and came to his father. But while he was yet at a distance, his father saw him and had compassion, and ran and embraced him and kissed him. And the son said to him, 'Father, I have sinned against heaven and before you; I am no longer worthy to be called your son.' But the father said to his servants, 'Bring quickly the best robe, and put it on him; and bring the fatted calf and kill it, and let us eat and make merry; for this my son was dead, and is alive again; he was lost, and is found.' And they began to make merry.

"Now his elder son was in the field; and as he came and drew near to the house, he heard music and dancing. And he called one of the servants and asked what

131

this meant. And he said to him, 'Your brother has come, and your father has killed the fatted calf, because he has received him safe and sound.' But he was angry and refused to go in. His father came out and entreated him, but he answered his father, 'Lo, these many years I have served you, and I never disobeyed your command; yet you never gave me a kid, that I might make merry with my friends. But when this son of yours came, who has devoured your living with harlots, you killed for him the fatted calf!' And he said to him, 'Son, you are always with me, and all that is mine is yours. It was fitting to make merry and be glad, for this your brother was dead, and is alive; he was lost, and is found.' ''

MEAT-FARE SUNDAY

Verse: The Lord is my strength and my song,
   The Lord has chastened me sorely.
The reading is from Paul's First Letter to the
   Corinthians.
Chapters 8.8-13; 9.1-2.
Brethren, food will not commend us to God. We are no worse off if we do not eat, and no better off if we do. Only take care lest this liberty of yours somehow becomes a stumbling block to the weak. For if any one sees you, a man of knowledge, at table in an idol's temple, might he not be encouraged, if his conscience is weak, to eat food offered to idols? And so by your knowledge this weak man is destroyed, the brother for whom Christ died. Thus, sinning against your brethren

132

and wounding their conscience when it is weak, you sin against Christ. Therefore, if food is a cause of my brother's failing, I will never eat meat, lest I cause my brother to fall.

Am I not free? Am I not an apostle? Have I not seen Jesus our Lord? Are not you my workmanship in the Lord? If to others I am not an apostle, at least I am to you; for you are the seal of my apostleship in the Lord.

THE GOSPEL READING
Matthew 25.31-46.

The Lord said: "When the Son of man comes in his glory, and all the angels with him, then he will sit on his glorious throne. Before him will be gathered all the nations, and he will separate them one from another as a shepherd separates the sheep from the goats, and he will place the sheep at his right hand, but the goats at the left. Then the King will say to those at his right hand, 'Come, O blessed of my Father, inherit the kingdom prepared for you from the foundation of the world; for I was hungry and you gave me food, I was thirsty and you gave me drink, I was a stranger and you welcomed me, I was naked and you clothed me, I was sick and you visited me, I was in prison and you came to me.' Then the righteous will answer him, 'Lord, when did we see you hungry and feed you, or thirsty and give you drink? And when did we see you a stranger and welcome you, or naked an clothe you? And when did we see you sick or in prison and visit you? And the King will answer them, 'Truly, I say to

133

you, as you did it to one of the least of these my brethren, you did it to me.' Then he will say to those at his left hand, 'Depart from me, you cursed, into the eternal fire prepared for the devil and his angels; for I was hungry and you gave me no food, I was thirsty and you gave me no drink, I was a stranger and you did not welcome me, naked and you did not clothe me, sick and in prison and you did not visit me.' Then they also will answer, 'Lord, when did we see you hungry or thirsty or a stranger or naked or sick or in prison, and did not minister to you?' Then he will answer them, 'Truly, I say to you, as you did it not to one of the least of these, you did it not to me.' And they will go away into eternal punishment, but the righteous into eternal life.''

CHEESE-FARE SUNDAY

Verse: Sing praises to our God, sing praises.
Clap your hands, all you nations.
The reading is from Paul's Letter to the Romans.
Chapters 13.11-14; 14.1-4.
Brethren, salvation is nearer to us now than when we first believed; the night is far gone, the day is at hand. Let us then cast off the works of darkness and put on the armor of light; let us conduct ourselves becomingly as in the day, not in reveling and drunkeness, not in debauchery and licentiousness, not in quarreling and jealousy. But put on the Lord Jesus Christ, and make no provision for the flesh, to gratify its desires.

As for the man who is weak in faith, welcome him,

but not for disputes over opinions. One believes he may eat anything, while the weak man eats only vegetables. Let not him who eats despise him who abstains, and let not him who abstains pass judgment on him who eats; for God has welcomed him. Who are you to pass judgment on the servant of another? It is before his own master that he stands or falls. And he will be upheld, for the Master is able to make him stand.

THE GOSPEL READING
Matthew 6.14-21.

The Lord said: "If you forgive men their trespasses, your heavenly Father will forgive you; but if you do not forgive men their trespasses, neither will your Father forgive your trespasses.

"And when you fast, do not look dismal, like the hypocrites, for they disfigure their faces that their fasting may be seen by men. Truly, I say to you, they have their reward. But when you fast, anoint your head and wash your face, that your fasting may not be seen by men but by your Father who is in secret; and your Father who sees in secret will reward you.

"Do not lay up for yourselves treasures on earth, where moth and rust consume and where thieves break in and steal. For where your treasure is, there will your heart be also."

FIRST SUNDAY IN LENT
SUNDAY OF ORTHODOXY

Verse: Blessed are you, O Lord, God of our Fathers.
For you are righteous in all things
you have done for us.
The reading is from Paul's Letter to the Hebrews.
Chapter 11.24-26, 32-40; 12.1-2.

Brethren, by faith Moses, when he was grown up, refused to be called the son of Pharoah's daughter, choosing rather to share ill-treatment with the people of God than to enjoy the fleeting pleasures of sin.

And what more shall I say? For time would fail me to tell of Gideon, Barak, Samson, Jephthah, of David and Samuel and the prophets—who through faith conquered kingdoms, enforced justice, received promises, stopped the mouths of lions, quenched raging fire, escaped the edge of the sword, won strength out of weakness, became mighty in war, put foreign armies to flight. Women received their dead by resurrection. Some were tortured, refusing to accept release, that they might rise again to a better life. Others suffered mocking and scourging, and even chains and imprisonment. They were stoned, they were sawn in two, they were killed with the sword; they went about in skins of sheep and goats, destitute, afflicted, ill-treated— of whom the world was not worthy—wandering over deserts and mountains, and in dens and caves of the earth.

And all these, though well attested by their faith, did not receive what was promised, since God had foreseen something better for us, that apart from us they should not be made perfect.

Therefore, since we are surrounded by so great a cloud of witnesses, let us also lay aside every weight, and sin which clings so closely, and let us run with perseverance the race that is set before us, looking to Jesus the pioneer and perfecter of our faith, who for the joy that was set before him endured the cross, despising the shame, and is seated at the right hand of the throne of God.

THE GOSPEL READING
John 1.43-52.

At that time, Jesus decided to go to Galilee. And he found Philip and said to him, "Follow me." Now Philip was from Bethsaida, the city of Andrew and Peter. Philip found Nathanael, and said to him, "We have found him of whom Moses in the law and also the prophets wrote, Jesus of Nazareth, the son of Joseph." Nathanael said to him, "Can anything good come out of Nazareth?" Philip said to him, "Come and see." Jesus saw Nathanael coming to him, and said of him, "Behold, an Israelite indeed, in whom is no guile!" Nathanael said to him, "How do you know me?" Jesus answered him, "Before Philip called you, when you were under the fig tree, I saw you." Nathanael answered him, "Rabbi, you are the Son of God! You are the King of Israel!" Jesus answered him, "Because I said to you, I saw you under the fig tree, do you believe? You shall see greater things than these." And he said to him, "Truly, truly, I say to you, you will see heaven opened, and the angels of God ascending and descending upon the Son of man.''

SECOND SUNDAY IN LENT

Verse: You, O Lord, shall keep us and preserve us.
Save me, O Lord,
for the godly man has failed.
The reading is from Paul's Letter to the Hebrews.
Chapters 1.10-14; 2.1-3.
"Thou, Lord, didst found the earth
in the beginning,
and the heavens are the work of thy hands;
they will perish, but Thou remainest;
they will all grow old like a garment, like a mantle
Thou wilt roll them up, and they will be changed.
But Thou art the same,
and thy years will never end.''
But to what angel has he ever said,
"Sit at my right hand, till I make thy enemies
a stool for thy feet?''
Are they not all ministering spirits sent forth to
serve, for the sake of those who are to obtain
salvation?

Therefore we must pay the closer attention to what
we have heard, lest we drift away from it. For if the
message declared by angels was valid and every trans-
gression or disobedience received a just retribution,
how shall we escape if we neglect such a great
salvation?

THE GOSPEL READING
Mark 2.1.12.

At that time, Jesus entered Capernaum and it was reported that he was at home. And many were gathered together, so that there was no longer room for them, not even about the door; and he was preaching the word to them. And they came, bringing to him a paralytic carried by four men. And when they could not get near him because of the crowd, they removed the roof above him; and when they had made an opening, they let down the pallet on which the paralytic lay. And when Jesus saw their faith, he said to the paralytic, "My son, your sins are forgiven." Now some of the scribes were sitting there, questioning in their hearts, "Why does this man speak thus? It is blasphemy! Who can forgive sins but God alone?" And immediately Jesus, perceiving in his spirit that they thus questioned within themselves, said to them, "Why do you question thus in your hearts? Which is easier, to say to the paralytic, 'Your sins are forgiven.' or to say, 'Rise, take up your pallet and walk?' But that you may know that the Son of man has authority on earth to forgive sins"—he said to the paralytic— "I say to you, rise, take up your pallet and go home." And he rose, and immediately took up the pallet and went out before them all; so that they were all amazed and glorified God, saying, "We never saw anything like this!"

THIRD SUNDAY IN LENT

Verse: O Lord, save your people and bless your inheritance.
To you, O Lord, have I cried, O my God.
The reading is from Paul's Letter to the Hebrews.
Chapters 4.14-16; 5.1-6.

Brethren, since we have a great high priest who has passed through the heavens, Jesus, the Son of God, let us hold fast our confession. For we have not a high priest who is unable to sympathize with our weaknesses, but one who in every respect has been tempted as we are, yet without sin.

For every high priest chosen from among men is appointed to act on behalf of men in relation to God, to offer gifts and sacrifices for sins. He can deal gently with the ignorant and wayward, since he himself is beset with weakness. Because of this he is bound to offer sacrifice for his own sins as well as for those of the people. And one does not take the honor upon himself, but is called by God, just as Aaron was.

So also Christ did not exalt himself to be made a high priest, but was appointed by him who said to him,
"Thou art my Son,
today I have begotten Thee";
as he says also in another place,
"Thou art a priest for ever,
after the order of Melchizedek."

THE GOSPEL READING
Mark 8.34-38; 9.1.

The Lord said: "If anyone wishes to come after me, let him deny himself and take up his cross and follow me. For whoever would save his life will lose it; and whoever loses his life for my sake and the gospel's will save it. For what does it profit a man, to gain the whole world and forfeit his life? For whoever is ashamed of me and my words in this adulterous and sinful generation, of him will the Son of man also be ashamed, when he comes in the glory of his Father with the holy angels." And he said to them, "Truly, I say to you, there are some standing here who will not taste death before they see the kingdom of God come with power."

FOURTH SUNDAY IN LENT

Verse: The Lord will give strength to his people.
　　　　Bring to the Lord, O sons of God,
　　　　bring to the Lord honor and glory.
The reading is from Paul's Letter to the Hebrews.
Chapter 6.13-20.

Brethren, when God made a promise to Abraham, since he had no one greater by whom to swear, he swore by himself, saying, "Surely I will bless you and multiply you." And thus Abraham, having patiently endured, obtained the promise. Men indeed swear by a greater than themselves, and in all their disputes an oath is final for confirmation. So when God desired to show more convincingly to the heirs of the promise the unchangeable character of his purpose, he interposed with an oath, so that through two unchangeable things, in which it is impossible that God should prove false, we who have field for refuge might have strong encouragement to seize the hope set before us. We have this as a sure and steadfast anchor of the soul, a hope that enters into the inner shrine behind the curtain, where Jesus has gone as a forerunner on our behalf, having become a high priest for ever after the order of Melchizedek.

THE GOSPEL READING
Mark 9.17-31.

At that time, a man came to Jesus kneeling and saying: "Teacher, I brought my son to you, for he has a dumb spirit; and wherever it seizes him, it dashes him down; and he foams and grinds his teeth and becomes rigid; and I asked your disciples to cast it out, and they were not able." And he answered them, "O faithless generation, how long am I to be with you? How long am I to bear with you? Bring him to me." And they brought the boy to him; and when the spirit saw him, immediately it convulsed the boy, and he fell on the ground and rolled about, foaming at the mouth. And Jesus asked his father, "How long has he had this?" And he said, "From childhood. And it has often cast him into the fire and into the water, to destroy him; but if you can do anything, have pity on us and help us." And Jesus said to him, "If you can! All things are possible to him who believes." Immediately the father of the child cried out and said,

142

"I believe; help my unbelief!" And when Jesus saw that a crowd came running together, he rebuked the unclean spirit, saying to it, "You dumb and deaf spirit, I command you, come out of him, and never enter him again." And after crying out and convulsing him terribly, it came out, and the boy was like a corpse; so that most of them said, "He is dead." But Jesus took him by the hand and lifted him up, and he arose. And when he had entered the house, his disciples asked him privately, "Why could we not cast it out?" And he said to them, "This kind cannot be driven out by anything but prayer and fasting."

They went on from there and passed through Galilee. And he would not have any one know it; for he was teaching his disciples, saying to them, "The Son of man will be delivered into the hands of men, and they will kill him; and when he is killed, after three days he will rise." But they did not understand the saying, and they were afraid to ask.

FIFTH SUNDAY IN LENT

Verse: Make your vows to the Lord
and perform them.
God is known in Judah; his name is great in Israel.
The reading is from Paul's Letter to the Hebrews.
Chapter 9.11-14.

Brethren, when Christ appeared as a high priest of the good things that have come, then through the greater and more perfect tent (not made with hands, that is, not of this creation) he entered once for all into the Holy Place, taking not the blood of goats and calves but his own blood, thus securing an eternal redemption. For if the sprinkling of defiled persons with the blood of goats and bulls and with the ashes of a heifer sanctifies for the purification of the flesh, how much more shall the blood of Christ, who through the eternal Spirit offered himself without blemish to God, purify your conscience from dead works to serve the living God.

THE GOSPEL READING
Mark 10.32-45.

At that time, Jesus taking the twelve again, he began to tell them what was to happen to him, saying, "Behold, we are going up to Jerusalem; and the Son of man will be delivered to the chief priests and the scribes, and they will condemn him to death, and deliver him to the Gentiles; and they will mock him, and spit upon him, and scourge him, and kill him; and after three days he will rise."

And James and John, the sons of Zebedee, came forward to him, and said to him, "Teacher, we want you to do for us whatever we ask of you." And he said to them, "What do you want me to do for you?" And they said to him, "Grant us to sit, one at your right hand and one at your left, in your glory." But Jesus said to them, "You do not know what you are asking. Are you able to drink the cup that I drink, or to be baptized with the baptism with which I am baptized?" And they said to him, "We are able." And Jesus said to them, "The cup that I drink you will drink; and with the baptism with which I am baptized,

144

you will be baptized; but to sit at my right hand or at my left is not mine to grant, but it is for those for whom it has been prepared.'' And when the ten heard it, they began to be indignant of James and John. And Jesus called them to him and said to them, ''You know that those who are supposed to rule over the Gentiles lord it over them, and their great men exercise authority over them. But it shall not be so among you; but whoever would be great among you must be your servant, and whoever would be first among you must be slave of all. For the Son of man also came not to be served but to serve, and to give his life as a ransom for many.''

PALM SUNDAY

Verse: Blessed is he who comes
in the name of the Lord.
Give thanks to the Lord, for he is good.
His mercy endures forever.
The reading is from Paul's Letter to the Philippians.
Chapter 4.4-9.
Brethren, rejoice in the Lord always; again I will say, Rejoice. Let all men know your forbearance. The Lord is at hand. Have no anxiety about anything, but in everything by prayer and supplication with thanksgiving let your requests be made known to God. And the peace of God, which passes all understanding, will keep your hearts and your minds in Christ Jesus. Finally, brethren, whatever is true, whatever is honorable, whatever is just, whatever is pure, whatever

145

is lovely, whatever is gracious, if there is any excellence, if there is anything worthy of praise, think about these things. What you have learned and received and heard and seen in me; and the God of peace will be with you.

THE GOSPEL READING
John 12.1-18.

Six days before Passover, Jesus came to Bethany, where Lazaros was, whom Jesus had raised from the dead. There they made him a supper; Martha served, and Lazaros was one of those at table with him. Mary took a pound of costly ointment of pure nard and anointed the feet of Jesus and wiped his feet with her hair; and the house was filled with the fragrance of the ointment. But Judas Iscariot, one of the disciples (he who was to betray him), said "Why was this ointment not sold for three hundred denarii and given to the poor?" This he said, not that he cared for the poor but because he was a thief, and as he had the money box he used to take what was put into it. Jesus said, "Let her alone, let her keep it for the day of my burial. The poor you always have with you, but you do not always have me."

When the great crowd of the Jews learned that he was there, they came, not only on account of Jesus but also to see Lazaros, whom he had raised from the dead. So the chief priests planned to put Lazaros also to death, because on account of him many of the Jews were going away and believing in Jesus.

The next day a great crowd who had come to the

feast heard that Jesus was coming to Jerusalem. So they took branches of palm trees and went out to meet him, crying, "Hosanna! Blessed is he who comes in the name of the Lord, even the King of Israel!" And Jesus found a young ass and sat upon it; as it is written,

"Fear not, daughter of Zion;
behold, your king is coming,
sitting on an ass's colt!"

His disciples did not understand this at first; but when Jesus was glorified, then they remembered that this had been written of him and had been done to him. The crowd that had been with him when he called Lazaros out of the tomb and raised him from the dead bore witness. The reason why the crowd went to meet him was that they heard he had done this sign.

SUNDAY BEFORE THE EXALTATION OF THE PRECIOUS AND LIFE-GIVING CROSS

O Lord, save Your people and bless Your inheritance.
Verse: To You, O Lord, have I cried, O my God.
The reading is from Paul's First Letter to the Galatians.
Chapter 6.11-18.

Brethren, see with what large letters I am writing to you with my own hand. It is those who want to make a good showing in the flesh that would compel you to be circumcised, and not only in order that they may not be persecuted for the cross of Christ. For even those who receive circumcision do not themselves keep the law, but they desire to have you circumcised that

147

they may glory in your flesh. But far be it from me to glory except in the cross of our Lord Jesus Christ, by which the world has been crucified to me, and I to the world. For neither circumcision counts for anything, nor uncircumcision, but a new creation. Peace and mercy be upon all who walk by this rule, upon the Israel of God.

Henceforth let no man trouble me; for I bear on my body the marks of Jesus.

The grace of our Lord Jesus Christ be with your spirit, brethren. Amen.

GOSPEL READING
John 3.13-17.

The Lord said: No one has ascended into heaven but he who descended from heaven, the Son of man who is in heaven. And as Moses lifted up the serpent in the wilderness, so must the Son of man be lifted up, that whoever believes in him may have eternal life.

For God so loved the world that he gave his only Son, that whoever believes in him should not perish but have eternal life. For God sent the Son into the world, not to condemn the world, but that the world might be saved through him.

THE UNIVERSAL EXALTATION OF THE PRECIOUS AND LIFE-GIVING CROSS

Exalt the Lord our God.
Verse: The Lord reigns; let the people tremble.
The reading is from Paul's First Letter to the Corinthians.

Chapter 1.18-24.

Brethren, the word of the cross is folly to those who are perishing, but to us who are being saved it is the power of God. For it is written, "I will destroy the wisdom of the wise, and the cleverness of the clever I will thwart." Where is the wise man? Where is the scribe? Where is the debater of this age? Has not God made foolish the wisdom of the world? For since, in the wisdom of God, the world did not know God through wisdom, it pleased God through the folly of what we preach to save those who believe. For Jews demand signs and Greeks seek wisdom, but we preach Christ crucified, a stumbling block to Jews and folly to Gentiles, but to those who are called, both Jews and Greeks, Christ the power of God and the wisdom of God.

THE GOSPEL READING
John 19.6-11, 13-20, 25-28, 30.

At that time, when the chief priests and the officers saw him, they cried out, "Crucify him, crucify him!" Pilate said to them, "Take him yourselves and crucify him, for I find no crime in him." The Jews answered him, "We have a law, and by that law he ought to die, because he has made himself the Son of God." When Pilate heard these words, he was the more afraid; he entered the praetorium again and said to Jesus, "Where are you from?" But Jesus gave no answer. Pilate therefore said to him, "You will not speak to me? Do you not know that I have the power to release you, and power to crucify you?" Jesus answered him, "You would have no power over me unless it had been given you from above; therefore he who delivered me to you has the greater sin."

When Pilate heard these words, he brought Jesus out and sat down on the judgment seat at a place called The Pavement, and in Hebrew, Gabbatha. Now it was the day of Preparation of the Passover; it was about the sixth hour. He said to the Jews, "Behold your King!" They cried out, "Away with him, away with him, crucify him!" The chief priests answered, "We have no king but Caesar." Then he handed him over to be crucified.

So they took Jesus, and he went out, bearing his own cross, to the place called the place of a skull, which is called in Hebrew Golgotha. There they crucified him, and with him two others, one on either side, and Jesus between them. Pilate also wrote a title and put it on the cross; it read, "Jesus of Nazareth, the King of the Jews." Many of the Jews read this title, for the place where Jesus was crucified was near the city; and it was written in Hebrew, in Latin, and in Greek.

But standing by the cross of Jesus were his mother, and his mother's sister, Mary the wife of Clopas, and Mary Magdalene. When Jesus saw his mother, and the disciple whom he loved standing near, he said to his mother, "Woman, behold your son!" Then he said to the disciple, "Behold, your mother!" And from that hour the disciple took her to his own home.

After this Jesus, knowing that all was now finished, bowed his head and gave up his spirit.

SUNDAY AFTER THE EXALTATION OF THE PRECIOUS AND LIFE-GIVING CROSS

O Lord, save Your people and bless Your inheritance. *Verse:* To You, O Lord, have I cried, O my God. The reading is from Paul's Letter to the Galatians. *Chapter 2.16-20.*

Brethren, you know that a man is not justified by works of the law but through faith in Jesus Christ, even we have believed in Christ Jesus, in order to be justified by faith in Christ, and not by works of the law, because by works of the law shall no one be justified. But if, in our endeavor to be justified in Christ, we ourselves were found to be sinners, is Christ then an agent of sin? Certainly not! But if I build up again those things which I tore down, then I prove myself a transgressor. For I through the law died to the law, that I might live to God. I have been crucified with Christ; it is no longer I who live, but Christ who lives in me; and the life I now live in the flesh I live by faith in the Son of God, who loved me and gave himself for me.

GOSPEL READING
Mark 8.34-38, 9.1

The Lord said, "If any man would come after me, let him deny himself and take up his cross and follow me. For whoever would save his life will lose it; and whoever loses his life for my sake and the gospel's will save it. For what does it profit a man, to gain the whole world and forfeit his life? For what can a man give

151

in return for his life? For whoever is ashamed of me and of my words in this adulterous and sinful generation, of him will the Son of man also be ashamed, when he comes in the glory of his Father with the holy angels.

And he said to them, "Truly, I say to you, there are some standing here who will not taste death before they see that the kingdom of God has come with power."

SUNDAY OF THE HOLY FATHERS

Blessed are You, O Lord, the God of our Fathers.
Verse: For You are just in all You have done.
The reading is from Paul's Letter to Titus.
Chapter 3.8-15.

Titus, my son, the saying is true. I desire you to insist on these things, so that those who have believed in God may be careful to apply themselves to good deeds; these are excellent and profitable to men. But avoid stupid controversies, genealogies, dissensions, and quarrels over the law, for they are unprofitable and futile. As for a man who is factious, after admonishing him once or twice, knowing that such a person is perverted and sinful; he is self-condemned.

When I send Artemas or Tychicos to you, do your best to come to me at Nicopolis, for I have decided to spend the winter there. Do your best to speed Zenas the lawyer and Apollos on their way; see that they lack nothing. And let our people learn to apply themselves to good deeds, so as to help cases of urgent need, and

152

not to be unfruitful.

All who are with me send greetings to you. Greet those who love us in the faith.

Grace be with you all. Amen.

THE GOSPEL READING
Luke 8.5-15.

The Lord said this parable: "A sower went out to sow his seed; and as he sowed, some fell along the path, and was trodden under foot, and the birds of the air devoured it. And some fell on the rock; and as it grew up, it withered away, because it had no moisture. And some fell among thorns; and the thorns grew with it and choked it. And some fell into good soil and grew, and yielded a hundredfold.

And when his disciples asked him what this parable meant, he said, "To you it has been given to know the secrets of the kingdom of God; but for others they are in parables, so that seeing they may not see, and hearing they may not understand. Now the parable is this: The seed is the word of God. The ones along the path are those who have heard; then the devil comes and takes away the word from their hearts, that they may not believe and be saved. And the ones on the rock are those who, when they hear the word, receive it with joy; but these have no root, they believe for a while and in time of temptation fall away. And as for what fell among the thorns, they are those who hear, but as they go on their way they are choked by the cares and riches and pleasures of life, and their fruit does not mature. And as for that in the good soil, they are those who, hearing the word, hold it fast in an honest and good heart, and bring forth fruit with patience. As he said these things, he cried out, "He who has ears to hear, let him hear."

THE HOLY THEOPHANY OF OUR LORD AND GOD AND SAVIOR JESUS CHRIST

Blessed is He who comes in the name of the Lord.
Verse: Give thanks to the Lord, for He is good.
The reading is from Paul's Letter to Titus.
Chapter 2.11-14, 3.4-7.

Titus, my son, the grace of God has appeared for the salvation of all men, training us to renounce irreligion and worldly passions, and to live sober, upright, and godly lives in this world, awaiting our blessed hope, the appearing of the glory of the great God and Savior Jesus Christ, who gave himself for us to redeem us from all iniquity and to purify for himself a people of his own who are zealous for good deeds.

Declare these things; exhort and reprove with all authority. Let no one disregard you.

But when the goodness and loving kindness of God our Savior appeared, he saved us, not because of deeds done by us in righteousness, but in virtue of his own mercy, by the washing of regeneration and renewal in the Holy Spirit, which he poured out upon us richly through Jesus Christ our Savior, so that we might be justified by his grace and become heirs in hope of eternal life.

154

THE GOSPEL READING
Matthew 3.13-17.

Then Jesus came from Galilee to the Jordan to John, to be baptized by him. John would have prevented him, saying, "I need to be baptized by you, and do you come to me?" But Jesus answered him, "Let it be so now; for thus it is fitting for us to fulfill all righteousness." Then he consented. And when Jesus was baptized, he went up immediately from the water, and behold, the heavens were opened and he saw the Spirit of God descending like a dove, and alighting on him; and lo, a voice from heaven, saying, "This is my beloved Son, with whom I am well pleased."

SUNDAY AFTER THEOPHANY

Let your mercy, O Lord, be upon us.
Verse: Rejoice in the Lord, O you righteous.
The reading is from Paul' Letter to the Ephesians.
Chapter 4.7-13.

Brethren, grace was given to each of us according to the measure of Christ's gift. Therefore it is said, "When he ascended on high he led a host of captives, and he gave gifts to men." (In saying, "He ascended," what does it mean but that he had also descended into the lower parts of the earth? He who descended is he who also ascended far above all the heavens, that he might fill all things.) And his gifts were that some should be apostles, some prophets, some evangelists, some pastors and teachers, to equip the saints for the

155

work of ministry, for building up the body of Christ, until we all attain to the unity of the faith and of the knowledge of the Son of God, to mature manhood, to the measure of the stature of the fullness of Christ.

GOSPEL READING
Matthew 4.12-17.

At that time, when Jesus heard that John had been arrested, he withdrew into Galilee; and leaving Nazareth he went and dwelt in Capernaum by the sea, in the territory of Zebulun and Naphtali, that what was spoken by the prophet Isaiah might be fulfilled: "The land of Zebulun and the land of Naphtali, toward the sea, across the Jordan, Galilee of the Gentiles—the people who sat in darkness have seen a great light, and for those who sat in the region and shadow of death light has dawned."

From that time Jesus began to preach, saying, "Repent, for the kingdom of heaven is at hand."

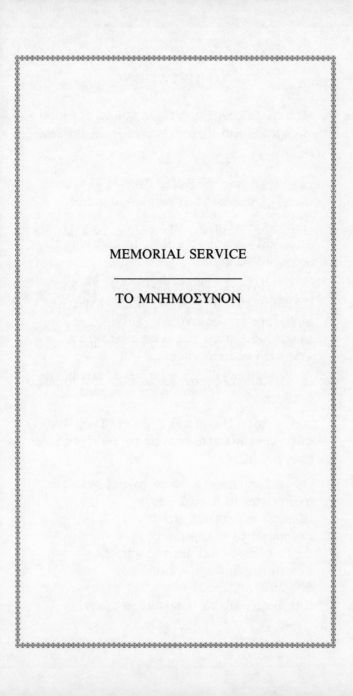

MEMORIAL SERVICE

ΤΟ ΜΝΗΜΟΣΥΝΟΝ

ΤΟ ΤΡΙΣΑΓΙΟΝ

Ἱερεύς: Εὐλογητὸς ὁ Θεὸς ἡμῶν, πάντοτε· νῦν καὶ ἀεὶ καὶ εἰς τοὺς αἰῶνας τῶν αἰώνων.

Λαός: Ἀμήν.

Λαός: Ἅγιος ὁ Θεός, Ἅγιος Ἰσχυρός, Ἅγιος Ἀθάνατος ἐλέησον ἡμᾶς (3).

Λαός: Δόξα Πατρὶ καὶ Υἱῷ καὶ Ἁγίῳ Πνεύματι· καὶ νῦν καὶ ἀεὶ καὶ εἰς τοὺς αἰῶνας τῶν αἰώνων. Ἀμήν.

Λαός: Παναγία Τριάς, ἐλέησον ἡμᾶς. Κύριε, ἱλάσθητι ταῖς ἁμαρτίαις ἡμῶν. Δέσποτα, συγχώρησον τὰς ἀνομίας ἡμῖν. Ἅγιε, ἐπίσκεψαι καὶ ἴασαι τὰς ἀσθενείας ἡμῶν, ἕνεκεν τοῦ ὀνόματός σου.

Λαός: Κύριε ἐλέησον· Κύριε, ἐλέησον· Κύριε, ἐλέησον.

Λαός: Δόξα Πατρὶ καὶ Υἱῷ καὶ Ἁγίῳ Πνεύματι· καὶ νῦν καὶ ἀεὶ καὶ εἰς τοὺς αἰῶνας τῶν αἰώνων. Ἀμήν.

Λαός: Πάτερ ἡμῶν, ὁ ἐν τοῖς οὐρανοῖς, ἁγιασθήτω τὸ ὄνομά σου.
Ἐλθέτω ἡ βασιλεία σου.
Γενηθήτω τὸ θέλημά σου,
ὡς ἐν οὐρανῷ καὶ ἐπὶ τῆς γῆς.
Τὸν ἄρτον ἡμῶν τὸν ἐπιούσιον
δὸς ἡμῖν σήμερον.
Καὶ ἄφες ἡμῖν τὰ ὀφειλήματα ἡμῶν,

THE TRISAGION

Priest: Blessed is our God, always, now and forever and to the ages of ages.

People: Amen.

People: Holy God, Holy Mighty, Holy Immortal, have mercy on us (3).

People: Glory to the Father and the Son and the Holy Spirit, now and forever and to the ages of ages. Amen.

People: All-holy Trinity, have mercy on us. Lord, forgive our sins. Master, pardon our transgressions. Holy One, visit and heal our infirmities for the glory of Your name.

People: Lord, have mercy. Lord, have mercy. Lord, have mercy.

People: Glory to the Father and the Son and the Holy Spirit, now and forever and to the ages of ages. Amen.

People: Our Father, who art in heaven,
hallowed by Thy name.
Thy kingdom come,
Thy will be done
on earth as it is in heaven.
Give us this day
our daily bread
and forgive our trespasses,

ὡς καὶ ἡμεῖς ἀφίεμεν τοῖς ὀφειλέταις ἡμῶν. Καὶ μὴ εἰσενέγκῃς ἡμᾶς εἰς πειρασμόν, ἀλλὰ ῥῦσαι ἡμᾶς ἀπὸ τοῦ πονηροῦ.

Ἱερεύς: ῞Οτι σοῦ ἐστιν ἡ βασιλεία καὶ ἡ δύναμις καὶ ἡ δόξα τοῦ Πατρὸς καὶ τοῦ Υἱοῦ καὶ τοῦ ῾Αγίου Πνεύματος, νῦν καὶ ἀεὶ καὶ εἰς τοὺς αἰῶνας τῶν αἰώνων.

Λαός: ᾿Αμήν.

Λαός: Μετὰ πνευμάτων δικαίων τετελειωμένων, τὴν ψυχὴν τοῦ δούλου *(τῆς δούλης)* σου, Σῶτερ, ἀνάπαυσον, φυλάττων αὐτὴν εἰς τὴν μακαρίαν ζωήν, τὴν παρὰ σοί, φιλάνθρωπε.

Λαός: Εἰς τὴν κατάπαυσίν σου, Κύριε, ὅπου πάντες οἱ ῞Αγιοί σου ἀναπαύονται, ἀνάπαυσον καὶ τὴν ψυχὴν τοῦ δούλου *(τῆς δούλης)* σου, ὅτι μόνος ὑπάρχεις ἀθάνατος.

Λαός: Δόξα Πατρὶ καὶ Υἱῷ καὶ ῾Αγίῳ Πνεύματι.

Λαός: Σὺ εἶ ὁ Θεὸς ἡμῶν, ὁ καταβὰς εἰς ῞Αδην καὶ τὰς ὀδύνας λύσας τῶν πεπεδημένων· αὐτὸς καὶ τὴν ψυχὴν τοῦ δούλου *(τῆς δούλης)* σου, Σῶτερ ἀνάπαυσον.

Λαός: Καὶ νῦν καὶ ἀεὶ καὶ εἰς τοὺς αἰῶνας τῶν αἰώνων. ᾿Αμήν.

Λαός: ῾Η μόνη ἁγνὴ καὶ ἄχραντος Παρθένος, ἡ Θεὸν ἀφράστως κυήσασα, πρέσβευε ὑπὲρ

as we forgive those who trespass against us.
And lead us not into temptation,
but deliver us from evil.

Priest: For Yours is the kingdom and the power
and the glory, of the Father and the Son and
the Holy Spirit, now and forever and to the
ages of ages.

People: Amen.

People: Among the spirits of the righteous
perfected in faith, give rest, O Savior, to the
soul of Your servant. Bestow upon it the
blessed life which is from You, O loving Lord.

People: Within Your peace, O Lord, where
all Your Saints repose, give rest also to the
soul of Your servant, for You alone are Immortal.

People: Glory to the Father and the Son and
the Holy Spirit.

People: O Savior, You are our God who descended into Hades and delivered from suffering those who were bound there. Grant rest also
to the soul of Your servant.

People: Now and forever and to the ages of
ages. Amen.

People: Most pure and spotless Virgin, who ineffably gave birth to God, intercede with Him

τοῦ σωθῆναι τὴν ψυχὴν τοῦ δούλου (τῆς δούλης) σου.

Ἱερεύς: Ἐλέησον ἡμᾶς ὁ Θεός, κατὰ τὸ μέγα
ἔλεός σου, δεόμεθά σου, ἐπάκουσον καὶ
ἐλέησον.

Λαός: Κύριε, ἐλέησον (3).

Ἱερεύς: Ἔτι δεόμεθα ὑπὲρ ἀναπαύσεως τῆς
ψυχῆς τοῦ κεκοιμημένου δούλου (τῆς κεκοιμημένης δούλης) τοῦ Θεοῦ (Ὄνομα) καὶ ὑπὲρ
τοῦ συγχωρηθῆναι αὐτῷ (αὐτῇ), πᾶν πλημμέλημα ἑκούσιόν τε καὶ ἀκούσιον.

Λαός: Κύριε, ἐλέησον (3).

Ἱερεύς: Ὅπως Κύριος ὁ Θεὸς τάξῃ τὴν
ψυχὴν αὐτοῦ (αὐτῆς), ἔνθα οἱ δίκαιοι ἀναπαύ-
ονται· τὰ ἐλέη τοῦ Θεοῦ, τὴν βασιλείαν τῶν
οὐρανῶν, καὶ ἄφεσιν τῶν αὐτοῦ (αὐτῆς)
ἁμαρτιῶν, παρὰ Χριστῷ τῷ ἀθανάτῳ βασιλεῖ
καὶ θεῷ ἡμῶν αἰτησώμεθα.

Λαός: Σοί, Κύριε.

Ἱερεύς: Τοῦ Κυρίου δεηθῶμεν.

Λαός: Κύριε, ἐλέησον.

Ἱερεύς: Ὁ Θεὸς τῶν πνευμάτων καὶ πάσης
σαρκός, ὁ τὸν θάνατον καταπατήσας, τὸν
δὲ διάβολον καταργήσας, καὶ ζωὴν τῷ κόσμῳ σου δωρησάμενος· αὐτὸς Κύριε ἀνάπαυσον τὴν ψυχὴν τοῦ κεκοιμημένου δούλου (τῆς

for the salvation of the soul of your servant.

Priest: Have mercy upon us, O God, according to Your great mercy; we pray to You, hear us and have mercy.

People: Lord, have mercy (*3*).

Priest: Again we pray for the repose of the soul of the departed servant of God (*Name*), and for the forgiveness of all his (*her*) sins, both voluntary and unvoluntary.

People: Lord, have mercy (*3*).

Priest: May the Lord God grant that his (*her*) soul rest where the righteous repose. Let us ask Christ, our immortal King and God, for the mercies of God, the kingdom of heaven, and the forgiveness of his (*her*) sins.

People: Grant this, O Lord.

Priest: Let us pray to the Lord.

People: Lord, have mercy.

Priest: O God of spirits and of all flesh, You have trampled upon death and have abolished the power of the devil, giving life to Your world. Give rest to the soul of Your departed

κεκοιμημένης δούλης) σου ἐν τόπῳ φωτεινῷ, ἐν τόπῳ χλοερῷ, ἐν τόπῳ ἀναψύξεως ἔνθα ἀπέδρα ὀδύνη , λύπη καὶ στεναγμός. Πᾶν ἁμάρτημα τὸ παρ᾽ αὐτοῦ (*αὐτῆς*) πραχθὲν ἐν λόγῳ ἢ ἔργῳ ἢ διανοίᾳ, ὡς ἀγαθὸς καὶ φιλάνθρωπος Θεὸς συγχώρησον· ὅτι οὐκ ἔστιν ἄνθρωπος ὃς ζήσεται καὶ οὐκ ἁμαρτήσει· σὺ γὰρ μόνος ἐκτὸς ἁμαρτίας ὑπάρχεις· ἡ δικαιοσύνη σου δικαιοσύνη εἰς τὸν αἰῶνα, καὶ ὁ λόγος σου ἀλήθεια.

Ἱερεύς: Ὅτι σὺ εἶ ἡ ἀνάστασις, ἡ ζωὴ καὶ ἡ ἀνάπαυσις τοῦ κεκοιμημένου δούλου (*τῆς κεκοιμημένης δούλης*) σου (Ὄνομα) Χριστὲ ὁ Θεὸς ἡμῶν καὶ σοὶ τὴν δόξαν ἀναπέμπομεν, σὺν τῷ ἀνάρχῳ σου Πατρί, καὶ τῷ παναγίῳ καὶ ἀγαθῷ καὶ ζωοποιῷ σου Πνεύματι, νῦν καὶ ἀεὶ καὶ εἰς τοὺς αἰῶνας τῶν αἰώνων. Ἀμήν.

Λαός: Δόξα Πατρὶ καὶ Υἱῷ καὶ Ἁγίῳ Πνεύματι· καὶ νῦν καὶ ἀεὶ καὶ εἰς τοὺς αἰῶνας τῶν αἰώνων. Ἀμήν.

Ἱερεύς: Δόξα σοι, ὁ Θεός, ἡ ἐλπὶς ἡμῶν, δόξα σοι.

Ἀπόλυσις

Ἱερεύς: Ὁ καὶ νεκρῶν καὶ ζώντων τὴν ἐξουσίαν ἔχων, ὡς ἀθάνατος Βασιλεύς, καὶ ἀναστὰς ἐκ νεκρῶν, Χριστὸς ὁ ἀληθινὸς Θεὸς ἡμῶν, ταῖς πρεσβείαις τῆς παναχράντου ἁγίας

servant (*Name*) in a place of light, in a place
of repose, in a place of refreshment, where
there is no pain, sorrow, and suffering. As a
good and loving God, forgive every sin he (*she*)
has committed in thought, word or deed, for
there is no one who lives and does not sin. You
alone are without sin. Your righteousness is an
everlasting righteousness, and Your word is
truth.

Priest: For You are the resurrection, the life,
and the repose of Your departed servant
(*Name*), Christ our God, and to You we give
glory, with Your eternal Father and Your all-
holy, good and life-giving Spirit, now and
forever and to the ages of ages. Amen.

People: Glory to the Father and the Son and
the Holy Spirit, now and forever and to the
ages of ages. Amen.

Priest: Glory to You, O God, our hope, glory
to You.

The Dismissal

Priest: May Christ our true God, who rose
from the dead and as immortal King has authority over the living and the dead, have mercy
on us and save us, through the intercessions of

αὐτοῦ μητρός· τῶν ἁγίων ἐνδόξων καὶ πανευφήμων Ἀποστόλων· τῶν ὁσίων καὶ θεοφόρων πατέρων ἡμῶν· τῶν ἁγίων ἐνδόξων προπατόρων Ἀβραὰμ Ἰσαὰκ καὶ Ἰακώβ· τοῦ ἁγίου καὶ δικαίου φίλου αὐτοῦ Λαζάρου τοῦ τετραημέρου, καὶ πάντων τῶν Ἁγίων, τὴν ψυχὴν τοῦ (τῆς) ἐξ ἡμῶν μεταστάντος (μεταστάσης) δούλου (δούλης) αὐτοῦ (αὐτῆς) ἐν σκηναῖς Δικαίων τάξαι, ἐν κόλποις Ἀβραὰμ ἀναπαῦσαι, καὶ μετὰ Δικαίων συναριθμῆσαι, ἡμᾶς δὲ ἐλεῆσαι ὡς ἀγαθὸς καὶ φιλάνθρωπος.

Ἱερεύς: Αἰωνία σου ἡ μνήμη, ἀξιομακάριστε καὶ ἀείμνηστε ἀδελφὲ ἡμῶν.

Ἐπὶ δὲ γυναικὸς·

Ἱερεύς: Αἰωνία σου ἡ μνήμη, ἀξιομακάριστος καὶ ἀείμνηστος ἀδελφὴ ἡμῶν.

Ἱερεύς: Δι’ εὐχῶν τῶν ἁγίων πατέρων ἡμῶν Κύριε Ἰησοῦ Χριστέ, ὁ Θεὸς ἡμῶν, ἐλέησον καὶ σῶσον ἡμᾶς.

Λαός: Ἀμήν.

his spotless holy Mother; of the holy, glorious, and praiseworthy Apostles; of our venerable and God-bearing Fathers; of the holy and glorious forefathers Abraham, Isaac, and Jacob; of his holy and righteous friend Lazaros, who lay in the grave four days; and of all the Saints, establish the soul of His servant (*Name*) departed from us, in the dwelling place of the Saints; grant rest to him (*her*) in the bosom of Abraham and number him (*her*) among the righteous.

Priest: May your memory be eternal, dear brother, worthy of blessedness and everlasting memory.

(*For women*)

Priest: May your memory be eternal, dear sister, worthy of blessedness and everlasting memory.

Priest: Through the prayers of our holy Fathers, Lord Jesus Christ, have mercy on us and save us.

People: Amen.

ΤΟ ΜΝΗΜΟΣΥΝΟΝ

Λαός: Εὐλογητὸς εἶ, Κύριε δίδαξόν με τὰ δικαιώματά σου.

Λαός: Τῶν ἁγίων ὁ χορός, εὗρεν πηγὴν τῆς ζωῆς καὶ θύραν Παραδείσου· εὕρω κἀγώ, τὴν ὁδὸν διὰ τῆς μετανοίας· τὸ ἀπολωλὸς πρόβατον ἐγὼ εἰμί· ἀνακάλεσαί με Σωτήρ, καὶ σῶσόν με.

Λαός: Εὐλογητὸς εἶ, Κύριε δίδαξόν με τὰ δικαιώματά σου.

Λαός: Ὁ πάλαι μέν, ἐκ μὴ ὄντων πλάσας με, καὶ εἰκόνι σου θείᾳ τιμήσας, παραβάσει ἐντολῆς δὲ πάλιν με ἐπιστρέψας, εἰς γῆν ἐξ ἧς ἐλήφθην· εἰς τὸ καθ᾽ ὁμοίωσιν ἐπανάγαγε, τὸ ἀρχαῖον κάλλος ἀναμορφώσασθαι.

Λαός: Εὐλογητὸς εἶ, Κύριε δίδαξόν με τὰ δικαιώματά σου.

Λαός: Εἰκὼν εἰμὶ τῆς ἀρρήτου δόξης σου, εἰ καὶ στίγματα φέρω πταισμάτων· οἰκτείρησον τὸ σὸν πλάσμα Δέσποτα, καὶ καθάρισον σῇ εὐσπλαγχνίᾳ· καὶ τὴν ποθεινὴν πατρίδα παράσχου μοι, Παραδείσου πάλιν ποιῶν πολίτην με.

Λαός: Εὐλογητὸς εἶ, Κύριε δίδαξόν με τὰ δικαιώματά σου.

Λαός: Ἀνάπαυσον ὁ Θεὸς τὸν δοῦλον (*τὴν δούλην*) σου, καὶ κατάταξον αὐτὸν (*αὐτὴν*) ἐν Παραδείσῳ, ὅπου χοροὶ τῶν ἁγίων Κύριε,

MEMORIAL SERVICE

People: Blessed are You, O Lord, teach me Your statutes.

People: The choir of Saints has found the fountain of life and the door of Paradise. May I also find the way through repentance. I am the sheep that is lost: O Savior, call me back and save me.

People: Blessed are You, O Lord, teach me Your statutes.

People: Of old You created me from nothing and honored me with Your divine image. But when I disobeyed Your commandment, O Lord, You cast me down to the earth from where I was taken. Lead me back again to Your likeness, and renew my original beauty.

People: Blessed are you, O Lord, teach me Your statutes.

People: I am an image of Your ineffable glory, though I bear the scars of my trangressions. On Your creation, Master, take pity and cleanse me by Your compassion. Grant me the homeland for which I long and once again make me a citizen of Paradise.

People: Blessed are You, O Lord, teach me Your statutes.

People: Give rest, O God, to Your servant, and place him (*her*) in Paradise where the choirs of the Saints and the righteous will shine as the

164

καὶ οἱ Δίκαιοι ἐκλάμψουσιν ὡς φωστῆρες· τὸν κεκοιμημένον δοῦλόν (*τὴν κεκοιμημένην δούλην*) σου ἀνάπαυσον, παρορῶν αὐτοῦ (*αὐτῆς*) πάντα τὰ ἐγκλήματα.

Λαός: Δόξα Πατρὶ καὶ Υἱῷ καὶ Ἁγίῳ Πνεύματι.

Λαός: Τὸ τριλαμπές, τῆς μιᾶς Θεότητος, εὐσεβῶς ὑμνήσωμεν βοῶντες· Ἅγιος εἶ ὁ πατὴρ ὁ ἄναρχος, ὁ συνάναρχος Υἱὸς καὶ θεῖον Πνεῦμα· φώτισον ἡμᾶς πίστει σοι λατρεύοντας καὶ τοῦ αἰωνίου πυρὸς ἐξάρπασον.

Λαός: Καὶ νῦν καὶ ἀεὶ καὶ εἰς τοὺς αἰῶνας τῶν αἰώνων.

Λαός: Χαῖρε σεμνή, ἡ Θεὸν σαρκὶ τεκοῦσα, εἰς πάντων σωτηρίαν, δι᾽ ἧς γένος τῶν ἀνθρώπων εὕρατο τὴν σωτηρίαν· διὰ σοῦ εὕρομεν Παράδεισον, Θεοτόκε ἁγνὴ εὐλογημένη.

Λαός: Ἀλληλούϊα, Ἀλληλούϊα, Ἀλληλούϊα, Δόξα σοι ὁ Θεός (3).

Ἦχος πλ. δ´.

Λαός: Μετὰ τῶν Ἁγίων ἀνάπαυσον, Χριστέ, τὴν ψυχὴν τοῦ δούλου σου (*τῆς δούλης σου*), ἔνθα οὐκ ἔστι πόνος, οὐ λύπη, οὐ στεναγμός, ἀλλὰ ζωὴ ἀτελεύτητος.

Ἦχος δ´.

Λαός: Μετὰ πνευμάτων δικαίων τετελειωμένων, τὴν ψυχὴν τοῦ δούλου σου (*τῆς δούλης*

stars of heaven. To Your departed servant give rest, O Lord, and forgive all his (*her*) offenses.

People: Glory to the Father and the Son and the Holy Spirit.

People: The threefold radiance of the one God let us praise, and let us shout in song: Holy are You, eternal Father, coeternal Son, and divine Spirit! Illumine us who worship You in faith and deliver us from the eternal fire.

People: Now and forever and to the ages of ages. Amen.

People: Rejoice, gracious Lady, who for the salvation of all gave birth to God in the flesh, and through whom the human race has found salvation. Through you, pure and blessed Theotokos, may we find Paradise.

People: Alleluia. Alleluia. Alleluia. Glory to You, O God (3).

Tone Eight
People: With the Saints give rest, O Christ, to the soul of Your servant where there is no pain, nor sorrow, nor suffering, but life everlasting.

Tone Four
People: Among the spirits of the righteous perfected in faith, give rest, O Savior, to the soul of Your servant. Bestow upon it the blessed life

σου), Σῶτερ ἀνάπαυσον, φυλάττων αὐτὴν εἰς τὴν μακαρίαν ζωὴν τὴν παρὰ σοί, φιλάνθρωπε.

Λαός: Εἰς τὴν κατάπαυσίν σου, Κύριε, ὅπου πάντες οἱ Ἅγιοί σου ἀναπαύονται, ἀνάπαυσον καὶ τὴν ψυχὴν τοῦ δούλου *(τῆς δούλης)* σου, ὅτι μόνος ὑπάρχεις ἀθάνατος.

Λαός: Δόξα Πατρὶ καὶ Υἱῷ καὶ Ἁγίῳ Πνεύματι.

Λαός: Σὺ εἶ ὁ Θεὸς ἡμῶν, ὁ καταβὰς εἰς Ἅδην καὶ τὰς ὀδύνας λύσας τῶν πεπεδημένων, αὐτὸς καὶ τὴν ψυχὴν τοῦ δούλου σου *(τῆς δούλης σου)*, Σῶτερ ἀνάπαυσον.

Λαός: Καὶ νῦν καὶ ἀεὶ καὶ εἰς τοὺς αἰῶνας τῶν αἰώνων.

Λαός: Ἡ μόνη ἁγνὴ καὶ ἄχραντος Παρθένος, ἡ Θεὸν ἀφράστως κυήσασα, πρέσβευε ὑπὲρ τοῦ σωθῆναι τὴν ψυχὴν τοῦ δούλου *(τῆς δούλης)* σου.

Ἱερεύς: Ἐλέησον ἡμᾶς ὁ Θεός, κατὰ τὸ μέγα ἔλεός σου, δεόμεθά σου, ἐπάκουσον καὶ ἐλέησον.

Λαὸς: Κύριε, ἐλέησον *(3)*.

Ἱερεύς: Ἔτι δεόμεθα ὑπὲρ ἀναπαύσεως τοῦ κεκοιμημένου δούλου *(τῆς κεκοιμημένης δούλης)* τοῦ Θεοῦ *(Ὄνομα)* καὶ ὑπὲρ τοῦ

which is from You, O loving One.

People: Within Your peace, O Lord, where all Your saints repose, give rest also to the soul of Your servant, for You alone are immortal.

People: Glory to the Father and the Son and the Holy Spirit.

People: You are our God who descended into Hades and loosened the pains of those who were chained. Grant rest also, O Savior, to the soul of Your servant.

People: Now and forever and to the ages of ages.

People: Most pure and spotless Virgin, who ineffably gave birth to God, intercede with Him for the salvation of the soul of your servant.

Priest: Have mercy upon us, O God, according to Your great love; we pray to You, hear us and have mercy.

People: Lord, have mercy (*3*).

Priest: Again we pray for the repose of the departed servant of God (*Name*) who has fallen asleep, and for the forgiveness of all his (*her*)

συγχωρηθῆναι αὐτῷ, πᾶν πλημμέλημα ἑκούσιόν τε καὶ ἀκούσιον.

Λαός: Κύριε, ἐλέησον (3).

Ἱερεύς: "Οπως Κύριος ὁ Θεὸς τάξῃ τὴν ψυχὴν αὐτοῦ (*αὐτῆς*), ἔνθα οἱ δίκαιοι ἀναπαύονται· τὰ ἐλέη τοῦ Θεοῦ, τὴν βασιλείαν τῶν οὐρανῶν, καὶ ἄφεσιν τῶν αὐτοῦ ἁμαρτιῶν, παρὰ Χριστῷ τῷ ἀθανάτῳ βασιλεῖ καὶ θεῷ ἡμῶν αἰτησώμεθα.

Λαός: Παράσχου, Κύριε.

Ἱερεύς: Τοῦ Κυρίου δεηθῶμεν.

Λαός: Κύριε, ἐλέησον.

Ἱερεύς: Ὁ Θεὸς τῶν πνευμάτων καὶ πάσης σαρκός, ὁ τὸν θάνατον καταπατήσας, τὸν δὲ διάβολον καταργήσας, καὶ ζωὴν τῷ κόσμῳ σου δωρησάμενος· αὐτὸς Κύριε ἀνάπαυσον τὴν ψυχὴν τοῦ κεκοιμημένου δούλου (*τῆς κεκοιμημένης δούλης*) σου (*"Ονομα*) ἐν τόπῳ φωτεινῷ, ἐν τόπῳ χλοερῷ, ἐν τόπῳ ἀναψύξεως ἔνθα ἀπέδρα ὀδύνη, λύπη καὶ στεναγμός. Πᾶν ἁμάρτημα τὸ παρ' αὐτοῦ πραχθὲν ἐν λόγῳ ἢ ἔργῳ ἢ διανοίᾳ, ὡς ἀγαθὸς καὶ φιλάνθρωπος Θεὸς συγχώρησον· ὅτι οὐκ ἔστιν ἄνθρωπος ὃς ζήσεται καὶ οὐκ ἁμαρτήσει· σὺ γὰρ μόνος ἐκτὸς ἁμαρτίας ὑπάρχεις· ἡ δικαιοσύνη σου δικαιοσύνη εἰς τὸν αἰῶνα, καὶ ὁ λόγος σου ἀλήθεια.

Ἱερεύς: "Οτι σὺ εἶ ἡ ἀνάστασις, ἡ ζωὴ καὶ

sins, both voluntary and unvoluntary.

People: Lord, have mercy (*3*).

Priest: May the Lord God place his (*her*) soul where the righteous repose. Let us ask for the mercies of God, the kingdom of Heaven, and the forgiveness of his (*her*) sins from Christ our immortal king and God.

People: Grant this, O Lord.

Priest: Let us pray to the Lord.

People: Lord, have mercy.

Priest: O God of spirits of all flesh, You have trampled down death and have abolished the power of the devil, giving life to Your world: Give rest to the soul of Your departed servant (*Name*) in a place of light, in a place of repose, in a place of refreshment, where there is no pain, sorrow, and suffering. As a good and loving God, forgive every sin he (*she*) committed in thought, word or deed, for there is no one who lives and is sinless. You alone are without sin. Your righteousness is an everlasting righteousness, and Your word is truth.

Priest: For You are the resurrection, the life

ἡ ἀνάπαυσις τοῦ κεκοιμημένου δούλου (*τῆς κεκοιμημένης δούλης*) σου (*Ὄνομα*) Χριστὲ ὁ Θεὸς ἡμῶν καὶ σοὶ τὴν δόξαν ἀναπέμπομεν, σὺν τῷ ἀνάρχῳ σου Πατρί, καὶ τῷ παναγίῳ καὶ ἀγαθῷ καὶ ζωοποιῷ σου Πνεύματι· νῦν καὶ ἀεὶ καὶ εἰς τοὺς αἰῶνας τῶν αἰώνων.

Λαός: Ἀμήν.

Λαός: Δόξα Πατρὶ καὶ Υἱῷ καὶ Ἁγίῳ Πνεύματι· νῦν καὶ ἀεὶ καὶ εἰς τοὺς αἰῶνας τῶν αἰώνων. Ἀμήν.

Ἀπόλυσις

Ἱερεύς: Δόξα σοι, ὁ Θεός, ἡ ἐλπὶς ἡμῶν, δόξα σοι.

Ἱερεύς: Ὁ καὶ νεκρῶν καὶ ζώντων τὴν ἐξουσίαν ἔχων, ὡς ἀθάνατος Βασιλεύς, καὶ ἀναστὰς ἐκ νεκρῶν, Χριστὸς ὁ ἀληθινὸς Θεὸς ἡμῶν, ταῖς πρεσβείαις τῆς παναχράντου ἁγίας αὐτοῦ μητρός· τῶν ἁγίων ἐνδόξων καὶ πανευφήμων Ἀποστόλων· τῶν ὁσίων καὶ θεοφόρων πατέρων ἡμῶν· τῶν ἁγίων ἐνδόξων προπατόρων Ἀβραάμ, Ἰσαὰκ καὶ Ἰακώβ· τοῦ ἁγίου καὶ δικαίου φίλου αὐτοῦ Λαζάρου τοῦ τετραημέρου, καὶ πάντων τῶν Ἁγίων, τὴν ψυχὴν τοῦ (*τῆς*) ἐξ ἡμῶν μεταστάντος (*μεταστάσης*) δούλου (*δούλης*) αὐτοῦ (*αὐτῆς*) ἐν σκηναῖς Δικαίων τάξαι, ἐν κόλποις Ἀβραὰμ ἀναπαῦσαι, καὶ μετὰ Δικαίων συναριθμῆσαι, ἡμᾶς δὲ ἐλεῆσαι ὡς ἀγαθὸς καὶ φιλάνθρωπος.

and the repose of Your departed servant (*Name*), Christ our God, and to You we give glory, with Your eternal Father and Your all-holy, good and life-giving Spirit, now and for-ever and to the ages of ages.

People: Amen.

People: Glory to the Father and the Son and the Holy Spirit, now and for ever and to the ages of ages. Amen.

The Dismissal

Priest: Glory to You, O God, our hope, glory to You.

Priest: May Christ our true God, who rose from the dead and as immortal King has authority over the living and the dead, have mercy on us and save us, through the inter-cessions of his spotless and holy Mother; of the holy, glorious, and praiseworthy Apostles; of our venerable and God-bearing Fathers; of the holy and glorious forefathers Abraham, Isaac, and Jacob; of his holy and righteous friend Lazaros, who lay in the grave four days; and of all the saints; establish the soul of His ser-vant (*Name*), departed from us, in the dwell-ing place of the saints; give rest to him in the bosom of Abraham and number him (*her*) among the righteous.

Λαός: Ἀμήν.

Ἱερεύς: Αἰωνία σου ἡ μνήμη, ἀξιομακάριστε καὶ ἀείμνηστε ἀδελφὲ ἡμῶν.

Ἐπὶ δὲ γυναικὸς·

Ἱερεύς: Αἰωνία σου ἡ μνήμη, ἀξιομακάριστη καὶ ἀείμνηστη ἀδελφὴ ἡμῶν.

Ἱερεύς: Δι' εὐχῶν τῶν ἁγίων πατέρων ἡμῶν Κύριε Ἰησοῦ Χριστέ, ὁ Θεὸς ἡμῶν, ἐλέησον καὶ σῶσον ἡμᾶς.

Λαός: Ἀμήν.

People: **Amen.**

Priest: May your memory be eternal, dear brother, for you are worthy of blessedness and everlasting memory.

(*For women*)

Priest: May your memory be eternal, dear sister, for you are worthy of blessedness and everlasting memory.

Priest: Through the prayers of our holy Fathers, Lord Jesus Christ, have mercy on us and save us.

People: **Amen.**

ΤΑ ΑΝΑΣΤΑΣΙΜΑ ΑΠΟΛΥΤΙΚΙΑ

Ἦχος α΄.

Τοῦ λίθου σφραγισθέντος ὑπὸ τῶν Ἰουδαίων, καὶ στρατιωτῶν φυλασσόντων τὸ ἄχραντόν Σου σῶμα, ἀνέστης τριήμερος Σωτήρ, δωρούμενος τῷ κόσμῳ τὴν ζωήν. Διὰ τοῦτο αἱ δυνάμεις τῶν οὐρανῶν ἐβόων σοι ζωοδότα· Δόξα τῇ ἀναστάσει σου Χριστέ, δόξα τῇ βασιλείᾳ σου, δόξα τῇ οἰκονομίᾳ σου, μόνε φιλάνθρωπε.

Ἦχος β΄.

Ὅτε κατῆλθες πρὸς τὸν θάνατον, ἡ ζωὴ ἡ ἀθάνατος, τότε τὸν ᾅδην ἐνέκρωσας, τῇ ἀστραπῇ τῆς θεότητος· ὅτε δὲ καὶ τοὺς τεθνεῶτας, ἐκ τῶν καταχθονίων ἀνέστησας, πᾶσαι αἱ δυνάμεις τῶν ἐπουρανίων ἐκραύγαζον· Ζωοδότα Χριστέ, ὁ Θεὸς ἡμῶν, δόξα σοι.

Ἦχος γ΄.

Εὐφραινέσθω τὰ οὐράνια, ἀγαλλιάσθω τὰ ἐπίγεια, ὅτι ἐποίησε κράτος, ἐν βραχίονι αὐτοῦ, ὁ Κύριος· ἐπάτησε τῷ θανάτῳ τὸν θάνατον· πρωτότοκος τῶν νεκρῶν ἐγένετο· ἐκ κοιλίας ᾅδου ἐρρύσατο ἡμᾶς, καὶ παρέσχε τῷ κόσμῳ τὸ μέγα ἔλεος.

170

THE RESURRECTION APOLYTIKIA

First Tone
Though the tomb was sealed by a stone and soldiers guarded Your pure body, You arose, O Savior, on the third day, giving life to the world. Therefore, O Giver of life, the heavenly powers praise You: Glory to Your resurrection, O Christ, glory to Your kingdom, glory to Your plan of redemption, O only loving God.

Second Tone
When you descended unto death, O life immortal, You destroyed Hades with the splendor of Your divinity. And when You raised the dead from the depths of darkness, all the heavenly powers shouted: O Giver of life, Christ our God, glory to You.

Third Tone
Let the heavens rejoice and earth be glad, for the Lord has shown the power of His reign: He has conquered death by death, and become the first born of the dead. He has delivered us from the depths of Hades; and has granted to the world great mercy.

Ἦχος δ´.

Τὸ φαιδρὸν τῆς Ἀναστάσεως κήρυγμα, ἐκ
τοῦ Ἀγγέλου μαθοῦσαι αἱ τοῦ Κυρίου μαθή-
τριαι, καὶ τὴν προγονικὴν ἀπόφασιν ἀπορ-
ρίψασαι, τοῖς Ἀποστόλοις καυχώμεναι ἔλε-
γον· Ἐσκυλεύεται ὁ θάνατος, ἠγέρθη Χριστὸς ὁ Θεός, δωρούμενος τῷ κόσμῳ τὸ μέγα ἔλεος.

Ἦχος πλ. α´.

Τὸν συνάναρχον Λόγον Πατρὶ καὶ Πνεύματι, τὸν ἐκ τῆς Παρθένου τεχθέντα εἰς σωτηρίαν ἡμῶν, ἀνυμνήσωμεν πιστοὶ καὶ προ-
σκυνήσωμεν· ὅτι ηὐδόκησε σαρκί, ἀνελθεῖν
ἐν τῷ σταυρῷ, καὶ θάνατον ὑπομεῖναι, καὶ
ἐγεῖραι τοὺς τεθνεῶτας, ἐν τῇ ἐνδόξῳ Ἀναστάσει αὐτοῦ.

Ἦχος πλ. β´.

Ἀγγελικαὶ Δυνάμεις ἐπὶ τὸ μνῆμά σου, καὶ
οἱ φυλάσσοντες ἀπενεκρώθησαν· καὶ ἵστατο
Μαρία ἐν τῷ τάφῳ, ζητοῦσα τὸ ἄχραντόν σου
σῶμα. Ἐσκύλευσας τὸν Ἅδην, μὴ πειρα-
σθεὶς ὑπ᾽ αὐτοῦ· ὑπήντησας τῇ παρθένῳ, δωρούμενος τὴν ζωήν. Ὁ ἀναστὰς ἐκ τῶν νεκρῶν, Κύριε δόξα σοι.

Fourth Tone

The joyful news of Your resurrection was told to the women disciples of the Lord by the angel. Having thrown off the ancestral curse, and boasting, they told the Apostles: death has been vanquished, Christ our God is risen, granting to the world great mercy.

Fifth Tone

To the Word, coeternal with the Father and the Spirit, born of the Virgin for our salvation, let us, the faithful, give praise and worship. Of His own will He mounted the cross in the flesh, He suffered death, and raised the dead by His glorious resurrection.

Sixth Tone

The heavenly powers appeared at Your tomb, and those guarding it became like dead. Mary stood at Your grave seeking Your pure body. You stripped the power of hades, not touched by its corruption. You met the virgin woman, as one who grants life. O Lord, who rose from the dead, glory to You.

Ἦχος βαρύς

Κατέλυσας τῷ Σταυρῷ σου τὸν θάνατον· ἠνέῳξας τῷ Λῃστῇ τὸν Παράδεισον· τῶν Μυροφόρων τὸν θρῆνον μετέβαλες· καὶ τοῖς σοῖς Ἀποστόλοις κηρύττειν ἐπέταξας· ὅτι ἀνέστης Χριστὲ ὁ Θεός, παρέχων τῷ κόσμῳ τὸ μέγα ἔλεος.

Ἦχος πλ. δ´

Ἐξ ὕψους κατῆλθες, ὁ εὔσπλαγχνος, ταφὴν κατεδέξω τριήμερον, ἵνα ἡμᾶς ἐλευθερώσῃς τῶν παθῶν. Ἡ ζωὴ καὶ ἡ ἀνάστασις ἡμῶν, Κύριε, δόξα σοι.

Seventh Tone

By Your cross You destroyed death, and to the thief You opened paradise. You transformed the sorrow of the Myrrhbearers, and commanded the Apostles to proclaim that You have risen from the dead, Christ our God, granting to the world great mercy.

Eighth Tone

From on high You descended, O merciful Lord, and accepted the three-day burial to free us from our passions. Glory to You, O Lord, our life and our resurrection.

ΤΩ ΘΕΩ ΔΟΞΑ

GLORY BE TO GOD